Best Kitchen Basics

Best Kitchen Basics

A CHEF'S COMPENDIUM FOR HOME

–

Mark Best

hardie grant books

—

As a cook and person, I have always valued authenticity over glib fashion. I guess this comes from my pragmatic Lutheran upbringing. The Lutheran church is a place of robust raw materials, wood, stone, linen, muted colour, rough hewn and real.

The Lutheran church was not a place of pomp or ceremony. Pastor Provey had many children and an Abraham Lincoln beard. Praise was faint and good works valued. I turned out basically agnostic but, while the indoctrination may not have stuck, the work ethic and aesthetic certainly have, which is to place value in the ordinary and find beauty in it.

My grandfather cultivated a large home garden. The beds had been turned over for two generations before him. He never bought seeds and never had. The loam was deep and black, nurtured by his rough hands, the shit of a thousand chickens and the compost of last year's crop. The garden was organic before that became a thing. Garlic started as hairy threads of green under glass and finished fermenting in papery, plaited bundles in the eaves of his shed. Tiny cucumbers, submerged under the weight of a faded plate and smooth stone, slowly bubbled. The ferment tempered by salt and pungent with dried dill.

My nanna cooked with exactness and efficiency. Her mother, my 'big nanna', would sit at the table beside her, tailing tiny green beans. Dinner always started with 'go and wash your hands', then tripe and onions might be served. The tall cupboard held a stack of coloured biscuit tins and the fridge smelled of mettwurst. These collective memories perhaps reek of cliché but they are mine and perhaps inform my work in the kitchen more than anything else. Good cooking is not about luxury ingredients nor should they be expensive or rare. It is a response to what you have, not what you want.

I had no burning ambition to be a chef. It just sort of happened. In hindsight I can see that cooking had always been a large part of my life. It just seemed so normal and, while it was enjoyed – sometimes celebrated – it was also a function of the everyday. We had fruit trees and chickens and a pet ram called Barney. Surfeit of the season meant I was well aware of how to preserve an apricot, plum and peach, what to do with a quince and what a feijoa was.

We would eat preserved fruit with supermarket ice cream until the fruiting season returned. That's what made it banal and why I think of it wistfully now. I would climb the fig trees, legs stinging from the nettles underneath and then I would put white fig sap on my warty thumb. I would eat almonds from when they were clear and jellied to when we would rattle the branches with bamboo canes to harvest the remainder. We had a rooster called Tom who finished his days as broth, his seven years on earth requiring a commensurate number of hours in the pot. We were made to eat him.

Like most Gen X kids, I walked home, seemingly miles, in my memory. The route had its rewards. Pomegranate trees on the first corner were turned into improvised machine-gun fire. I knew the fruit was edible but we never actually ate them. It was much more fun to spray a mouthful of seeds at my sister. The staccato fire and 'blood' splatter never got old. Neither did her screams of outrage. For some reason the burghers of my home town had lined the streets with plum trees. We would eat them from the first belly-rumbling blush of ripeness until they started to ferment on the branch under full sun. Of course this is just nostalgia, but it defined a memory of what things should taste like.

Cooking is not an art that relies on products accessible only to the professional chef. It's not just about technique but new and old thought; changing the context. Using the self-imposed parameters of the ubiquitous and everyday as a source of creativity has allowed me to reinvent something as ordinary as honeycomb. I use the same recipe components as your mum did. Professional curiosity and focus on detail have taken it to a different level. Using honey from the blue gum forests surrounding Sydney and our crème fraîche creates a dish from 'only' two elements.

The art of cooking is to take any ingredient and turn it into something beautiful, to make a silk purse out of a sow's ear. It is minimalism at its most delicious. A good cook can compose a menu walking through a supermarket (at least with the 20 per cent of food stuffs they stock that actually are edible). Salad onions have their own beauty and in good hands can be elevated beyond the ordinary. A parsnip usually relegated to the roasting pan or soup pot can sing as dessert when transformed with common builder's lime. Buy things in full season. When they are at their best, most abundant and their cheapest. This is the golden triangle of cooking. It's an egalitarian approach that eschews the inherent elitism and privilege I see creeping into the dialogue surrounding 'good food'.

This is a collection of everyday ingredients, in alphabetical order, with three recipes each. This is a selection of the basic recipes and techniques that I have developed over my 25-year career as a chef – 16 of those at Marque, and all of them as a very keen home cook. They are not your usual home recipes, but they are mine. Take them, use them, make them your own and part of your repertoire.

Happy cooking.

Mark

KITCHEN NOTES

All eggs are free-range and 55 g (2 oz)

All poultry is free-range

Cooking chocolate should be best-quality couverture chocolate

Oven temperatures are given for fan-forced ovens. For conventional ovens, increase the temperature by 20°C (35°F).

Generally speaking, the better your ingredients are, the better the result of your dish. Buy the best you can afford.

CHAPTER ONE

—

Apples

Apple sauce

— Makes 400 ml (13½ fl oz)

This recipe uses the most basic commodity apple – the granny smith. This version can feed Baby or you can serve it with roast pork. It is a blank canvas, which can be adapted to suit your needs, taste or, dare I say, proficiency? Using this recipe as the foundation, try different types of apples with different levels of sweetness, acidity and tannin. You can also try other varieties of sugar, or spices like star anise or fennel – even salted butter brings a certain something to the mix. The same recipe and rationale applies to pears or fennel when in season.

---

4 granny smith apples, peeled and cored

100 g (3½ oz) salted butter

2 cloves

1 cinnamon stick

1 piece mace (if you can't find this, try harder)

1 allspice berry

1 bay leaf

juice of 1 lemon

2 teaspoons sugar

Put the apples in a small saucepan with the butter, spices and bay leaf. Add the lemon juice, sugar and 2 tablespoons water. Cover with a tight-fitting lid and cook over low heat for 10–15 minutes or until the apples soften completely.

Remove the pan from the heat and discard the spices and bay leaf. Using a hand-held blender, blend the apples to a fine purée. Set aside until ready to use or store in an airtight jar or container in the refrigerator for up to 5 days.

Make this sauce in larger quantities and freeze in portions using resealable sandwich bags. Don't forget to label them, as freezing brings a certain anonymity. For a sweeter version double the sugar.

Shrunken apples

— Serves 4

By any other name this is a baked apple.

I guess the idea of builder's lime sounds unusual and, perhaps for the more delicate, intimidating. For context, let me assuage your fears and say that the Aztecs and Mayans used this basic method for some millennia and if we want to get technical, it is called nixtamalisation. It is a process used in the preparation of maize or corn, involving naturally occurring lime. This alkaline process allows the grain to be more easily ground and also greatly increases its nutritional value and produces the humble, but important, tortilla. For our purposes, the lime water reacts with the pectin of most fruits and vegetables to produce a fine leathery layer with, in the case of the apple, a concentrated, delicious centre. These are excellent with roast pork.

---

110 g (4 oz) lime powder (builder's hydrated lime)

1.125 litres (38 fl oz/4½ cups) filtered water

4 golden delicious apples

custard or vanilla ice cream to serve (optional)

Mix the lime powder with the filtered water, being careful not to inhale the lime, and place in the refrigerator overnight. The lime will sink to the bottom of the container.

The next day, decant the water and discard the lime sludge.

Peel the apples, leaving the stem in place if desired, and put them in the lime water. Leave to soak for 24 hours.

Preheat the oven to 140°C (275°F).

Wash the apples thoroughly under cold running water and pat them dry. Place them on a wire rack on a baking tray. Allow enough room between the apples for even drying. Bake for 2 hours, opening the oven every 15 minutes to release any steam build-up and to rotate the tray. Serve the apples with custard or vanilla ice cream if desired.

Builder's lime can be purchased at any hardware store. An incidental point: brickies love tacos.

Tarte tatin

— Serves 4

This tart should be attempted, practised and perfected. It isn't particularly difficult but does benefit from a caring touch. You can use supermarket pastry but it is so much better using our puff pastry recipe, which makes enough for two tarts.

8 large new-season fuji or delicious apples (10 if they are small)

150 g (5½ oz) butter, cubed

230 g (8 oz/1 cup) caster (superfine) sugar

juice of 1 orange

Crème fraîche (page 103) to serve

PUFF PASTRY

600 g (1 lb 5 oz) French unsalted butter

750 g (1 lb 11 oz) baker's flour

15 g (½ oz) table salt

300 g (10½ oz) butter, diced and softened

200 ml (7 fl oz) milk

200 ml (7 fl oz) pouring (single/light) cream

Please be careful turning the tart onto the serving platter, as the caramel is as forgiving as lava. Any offcuts of pastry can be used to make cheesy pastry twists.

To make the puff pastry, line a 15 cm (6 in) square mould with plastic wrap. Press the French unsalted butter into the mould and allow to harden in the refrigerator.

Combine the flour and salt in the bowl of a stand mixer fitted with the dough hook. Add the diced, softened butter and mix on low speed until you have a crumb-like texture. Add the milk and cream and mix to combine. Mix for a further 6 minutes. Remove the dough from the mixer, form it into a ball, wrap in plastic wrap and refrigerate for 2 hours.

Remove the moulded butter from the refrigerator. It should remain cold with some plasticity. Flatten the ball of dough slightly. Starting from the centre, roll a portion of the dough upwards to form a 'petal'. Rotate the dough 90 degrees and repeat. Do this until there are four petals. Place the moulded butter in the middle of the dough flower and fold each 'petal' over the butter like an envelope. It is important for the butter and the dough to be at a similar consistency – this means the dough may need to be refrigerated during the process; likewise the butter.

Once the butter is covered by the dough, roll it into a 30 × 45 cm (12 × 18 in) rectangle, ensuring the butter does not split out from the dough. Place the dough lengthways in front of you and, starting from the bottom, fold one-third into the middle. Then, from the top, fold the top third down to the middle. Turn the dough so the short side is on your left. Roll out again to 30 × 45 cm and repeat the folding process. This is one turn. Refrigerate the dough for 30 minutes. Repeat the process of rolling, folding and resting a further five times. The butter should be layered evenly throughout the dough with none breaking through the sides. It is important to work quickly so the dough remains chilled while rolling.

Preheat the oven to 180°C (350°F). Roll out 500 g (1 lb 2 oz) of the pastry on a lightly floured work surface to 5 mm (¼ in) thick. Cut out a rough 40 cm (16 in) circle, put it on a tray and refrigerate until required.

Peel and halve the apples. Use a melon baller to remove the core.

Place a heavy-based, ovenproof frying pan over medium–high heat. Add the butter and sugar and cook until a dark golden caramel forms. Add the orange juice and swirl to amalgamate. Place the apples, round side down, around the outside of the pan, overlapping them until you complete the circle. Fill the middle, crowding the apples as much as possible. You may need to add another or just a half. Working quickly (as the heat will melt the pastry), place the pastry disc on top of the apples, tucking the sides down under the outer row of apples. Prick half a dozen holes in the pastry. Bake for 45–60 minutes or until the pastry is dark golden. Remove from the oven and rest for 5 minutes. Place a large serving platter on top of the pan. With one hand on the base of the platter, use your other hand to pick up the pan and carefully flip it over. Lift off the pan. Serve the tart with crème fraîche.

CHAPTER TWO

—

Beef

Beef tartare

— Serves 4

Tartare is a ubiquitous menu staple and can be delicious when prepared well. My version of the classic puts new tyres on it and takes it for a spin. Tabasco is replaced by Sriracha, a delicious condiment that originated in Thailand but found fame in the Huy Fong foods 'rooster' brand created and manufactured in California by a Vietnamese refugee – it's a funny old world.

The other spices and condiments follow the theme and produce a dish of charming heat and umami. This could be served as an appetiser, main or beer snack.

---

400 g (14 oz) best-quality grass-fed beef (dry-aged rump for preference)

1 small red onion, finely chopped

½ bunch of garlic chives, finely chopped

2 teaspoons Sriracha sauce

½ teaspoon freshly ground black pepper

¼ teaspoon Sichuan pepper

1 teaspoon sea salt

4 best-quality, free-range egg yolks

Potato chips (page 197) to serve (optional)

Using a very sharp kitchen knife, coarsely mince (grind) the beef.

Combine the onion, chives and beef with the Sriracha sauce, black pepper, Sichuan pepper and salt. Mix well. Divide the tartare between four serving plates. Either sit the egg yolk on top of the tartare or stir it through until thoroughly combined. Serve with home-made potato chips, if desired.

Sichuan pepper in quantity has the numbing effect of a dentist's conversation.

Corned beef

— *Serves 4–6, plus sandwiches*

As a reminder of Australia's colonial past and the fact that domestic refrigeration dates from the 1950s, there is no better dish than corned beef. The English and French colonised a large part of the planet with this simple product. 'Corned' references salt 'corns', which were used to preserve beef for long periods at sea under sail. During the world wars it was also known as 'bully' beef – a corruption of the French word **bouillon,** *meaning 'to boil'. This method of preservation is a useful technique for secondary cuts to improve their texture and flavour. The red colour comes from the preservative saltpetre. Long, slow cooking yields a succulent cut and a symbiotic relationship develops with the vegetables in the pot.*

---

1 kg (2 lb 3 oz) corned silverside or tri-tip for preference

2 large carrots, peeled and halved

2 large onions, halved

1 celery stalk

a few fresh bay leaves

3 cm (1¼ in) piece fresh ginger

6 cloves

1 cinnamon stick

2 teaspoons black peppercorns

20 g (¾ oz) butter

20 g (¾ oz) plain (all-purpose) flour

20 g (¾ oz) dijon mustard

PARSLEY POTATOES

200 g (7 oz) new potatoes

20 g (¾ oz) butter

freshly ground black pepper

30 g (1 oz/½ cup) chopped curly parsley

Put the meat in a heavy-based saucepan and cover with water. Bring to the boil and then drain.

Rinse the saucepan and put the meat back in. Cover with fresh water and bring to a low simmer over medium–low heat. Add the vegetables, herbs and spices and cook gently for 1½–2 hours until a skewer can be inserted into the meat with only a little resistance.

When the meat is nearly done, cook the potatoes. Use some of the cooking liquor from the meat to cook the potatoes, skin on, for 15–20 minutes. When they are tender, toss them in the butter, freshly ground black pepper and the parsley and then transfer them to a warm serving dish.

Heat the butter and flour in a small saucepan over medium heat and cook until the mixture turns golden. Remove the pan from the heat and whisk in a little of the meat cooking liquor. Return to the heat and whisk in another 250 ml (8½ fl oz/1 cup) of the liquor. Cook until it thickens with a shine, then whisk in the mustard. Pour the sauce into a sauce boat to serve.

Slice the beef and serve it in deep bowls with the sauce, carrots, onions and the parsley potatoes.

Blanching the meat reduces the salt content of the final dish and produces a useful bouillon. Different cuts of beef have different cooking qualities, so do ask your butcher's opinion and weigh that against your own.

Beef daube

— Serves 4

There is this thing that happens in English, where brands are so commonplace they become a common noun or verb: bandaid, yoyo, hoover, granola are some examples. So it is with cooking and the French, where the cooking vessel becomes the name of the dish – casserole, poêle and, as in this case, daube, which is a terracotta cooking vessel from Provence.

---

1 kg (2 lb 3 oz) beef shin

100 g (3½ oz/⅔ cup) plain (all-purpose) flour

100 ml (3½ fl oz) olive oil

200 g (7 oz) pancetta or lardon (skin on), cut into 8 pieces

4 large carrots, peeled and cut into large chunks

12 small onions, outer layer of skin removed

1 bottle Shiraz

1 litre (34 fl oz/4 cups) chicken stock

3 fresh bay leaves

2 cinnamon sticks

½ bunch of thyme

1 vanilla bean

2 allspice berries

2 cloves

1 teaspoon black peppercorns

1 garlic bulb

zest of 1 orange

2 teaspoons cornflour (cornstarch)

Cut the beef shin into eight large pieces and dust them in the flour.

In a large, deep, heavy-based frying pan over medium heat, brown the beef on all sides in the olive oil. Drain and transfer the meat to a large ovenproof casserole.

Brown the pancetta in the same frying pan. Add it to the casserole, reserving the fat in the frying pan.

Brown the carrot in the frying pan then add it to the casserole.

Brown the onions in the frying pan and add them to the casserole, along with the remaining pancetta fat.

Pour the bottle of wine into the frying pan and cook over high heat until it has reduced to a syrup. Add the stock, bring to the boil and then add the contents of the pan to the casserole.

Preheat the oven to 120°C (250°F).

Tie the bay leaves, cinnamon, thyme and vanilla bean into a tight bundle using butcher's string then add it to the casserole with the remaining spices, garlic bulb and orange zest. Put the lid on the casserole and cook in the oven for 4–5 hours until the beef is gelatinous and just starting to fall apart.

Whisk the cornflour with 1 tablespoon cold water to make a slurry. Stir the slurry into the casserole over low heat until it thickens. Serve the daube in the casserole at the table.

—

CHAPTER THREE

Broccoli

Roast broccoli

— Serves 4

Conventional thought rarely yields surprises. This underrated vegetable suffers from a lack of endeavour and imagination in most kitchens. Steamed or stir-fried seems to be its common fate. Most things can be improved with time in a hot oven, some fat and the correct seasoning. Broccoli benefits more than most, with the oven releasing its umami potential.

---

2 heads broccoli

50 ml (1¾ fl oz) virgin olive oil

½ teaspoon dried chilli flakes

freshly ground black pepper

Murray River pink salt

zest and juice of ½ lemon

Peel the skin from the broccoli stems and cut the whole heads of broccoli lengthways into quarters.

Preheat the oven to 180°C (350°F).

Put the broccoli in a heavy baking dish and splash over the olive oil. Season with the chilli, pepper and pink salt to taste. Bake for 15–20 minutes until the broccoli is golden brown.

Just before serving, add the lemon zest and a good squeeze of the juice.

You can roast the lemon half with the broccoli and then squeeze the juices over the cooked broccoli. This deliciousness can be compounded by the addition of a good dash of fine balsamic vinegar. Also try roasting broccolini, kale or cavalo nero for similar gustatory splendour.

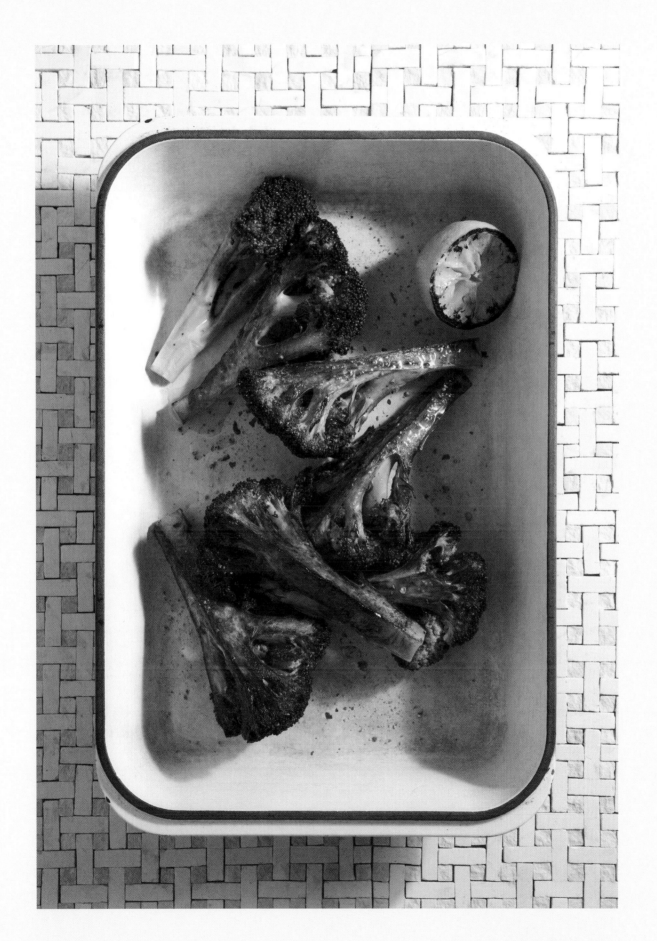

Orecchiette with broccoli

— Serves 4

Orecchiette or 'little ears' originated in Apulia in southern Italy. Like most things, they were originally hand-made but are now made by machine because nonnas are in short supply and too expensive to run. Look out for 100 per cent durum wheat pasta, made with bronze dies and air-dried for the best quality. Orecchiette is traditionally, and particularly good, served with turnip tops or cime di rapa. It is non-traditional to use butter as it is a southern dish, but sometimes butter tastes better.

---

2 heads broccoli

400 g (14 oz) durum wheat orecchiette

100 g (3½ oz) salted butter

2 garlic cloves, finely chopped

freshly ground black pepper

4 oregano sprigs, leaves picked

100 g (3½ oz) aged pecorino, finely grated

Peel the stems of the broccoli and remove the dried end. Thinly slice the broccoli.

Bring 3 litres (101 fl oz/12 cups) water to the boil in a large saucepan and add a handful of salt. Add the orecchiette and simmer until al dente (follow the packet instructions).

Heat the butter in a large frying pan until foaming. Add the garlic and broccoli and season well with pepper. Toss over high heat until the broccoli starts to colour.

Drain the pasta and add it to the pan with the oregano. Toss well and serve sprinkled with the pecorino.

Cook the orecchiette carefully as there is a fine line between 'little ears' and porridge.

Broccoli mole

— Serves 4

It is interesting to note the rise and rise of Latin America in culinary influence, indigenous home to the potato, tomato and most of the nightshade family. It is through the fame and talent of chefs like Enrique Olvera (Mexico), Gastón Acurio (Peru) and Alex Atala (Brazil) that we are realising the true depth of this culinary landscape.

This lovely condiment came from simply thinking 'broccoli mole sounds good'. Some research on the history of mole, or 'sauce' in Spanish, was revelatory. This version is based on a classic green mole and defies restraint following the first spoonful. I'll dedicate its birth to the wonderful Enrique Olvera, who once graced my kitchen. This is delicious with pan-fried fish, roasted or poached chicken, corned beef or even crackers.

BASE

30 g (1 oz/¼ cup) pepitas (pumpkin seeds)

50 g (1¾ oz/⅓ cup) sesame seeds

1 clove

2 allspice berries

2 teaspoons black peppercorns

30 ml (1 fl oz) sherry vinegar

1 teaspoon fine salt

GREEN PURÉE

100 g (3½ oz/2¼ cups) baby English spinach

2 spring onions (scallions), green part only

½ bunch of coriander (cilantro), leaves picked

1 garlic clove

1 jalapeño

CARAMELISED BROCCOLI

1 head broccoli

1 teaspoon fine salt

1 tablespoon olive oil

To make the base, in a dry frying pan over medium heat, toast the pepitas and sesame seeds until lightly brown. Add the clove, allspice and peppercorns and cook until aromatic. Grind the spices and seeds using an electric spice grinder or mortar and pestle. When a thick paste starts to form, add the sherry vinegar and 90 ml (3 fl oz) water, slowly, to emulsify. Add the salt and pulse (or grind) to combine.

To make the green purée, bring a large saucepan of water to a rapid boil. Blanch the spinach for 10 seconds. Use a slotted spoon to immediately transfer the spinach to a bowl of iced water. Repeat this process with the spring onion and then the coriander leaves. Strain through a fine sieve. In a food processor, blend the spinach, spring onion and coriander to a fine paste with the garlic, jalapeño and 200 ml (7 fl oz) cold water.

To make the caramelised broccoli, preheat the oven to 200°C (400°F).

Peel the broccoli stem then coarsely chop it together with the florets. Transfer to a baking tray and season with salt and olive oil. Roast for 10–15 minutes until caramelised. Cool.

Transfer the broccoli to a food processor and pulse several times to yield a bright green, chunky paste.

To assemble, mix together the base with the green purée and caramelised broccoli until well combined.

CHAPTER FOUR

—

Cabbage

Stuffed cabbage

— *Serves 6–8*

I don't think there is a country in Europe that wouldn't have some version of stuffed cabbage. A lot of them use the leaves to stuff and serve as small parcels. I like them but I prefer this version where the whole cabbage takes on a noble status to be carved like a Sunday roast.

---

1 small savoy cabbage

800 g (1 lb 12 oz) diced pork shoulder

200 g (7 oz) chicken livers

700 g (1 lb 9 oz) skinless, boneless chicken thighs

400 g (14 oz) pork back fat

2 celery stalks

1 bunch of tarragon

2 teaspoons sweet paprika

½ teaspoon ground coriander

½ teaspoon ground allspice

½ teaspoon freshly grated nutmeg

1 teaspoon white pepper

25 g (1 oz) salt

2 eggs

2 litres (68 fl oz/8 cups) chicken stock

Remove the core of the cabbage with a small, sharp knife. Carefully deconstruct the cabbage, being mindful not to tear the leaves – stop when you get to the pale core.

Bring a large saucepan of water to the boil and season with salt to the tune of 40 g (1½ oz) salt per litre (34 fl oz/4 cups) water.

Fill another saucepan of the same size with iced water.

Blanch the cabbage leaves in the boiling water, a few at a time, then immediately refresh them in the iced water. Drain the leaves on paper towel and leave to dry.

Put all of the meats and the celery through a coarse mincer (grinder).

Chop the tarragon and add it to the meat along with the spices, salt and eggs. Mix well with your hands.

Starting with the inner cabbage leaves, smear some of the stuffing on the inside of each leaf and rebuild the cabbage. Try to keep the leaves in their natural order for the best result.

Place the cabbage on a large square of muslin (cheesecloth). Bring the sides up and tie them at the top with butcher's string to form a tight, round parcel. Place in a large saucepan and cover with the chicken stock – top up with a little water if required. Bring to a low simmer and cook gently for 1 hour 45 minutes. The internal temperature should be 75°C (167°F) when cooked. Remove the cabbage from the pan and untie the muslin. Reserve the cooking liquor.

Serve in a large deep dish and carve at the table. Bowls of the cooking liquor can be served to start the meal.

The celery is important, not just for flavour, but because it contains high levels of nitrate, which will help retain the stuffing's rosy hue.

Roast brussels sprouts

— Serves 4

Ah, brussels sprouts. Was there ever a vegetable more maligned or abused by well-intentioned mothers? I've spent a career in re-educating my adoring public on the real beauty of this midget cabbage. Brussels sprouts are actually quite versatile and respond eloquently to not having the shit boiled out of them. No bi-carb required.

500 g (1 lb 2 oz) brussels sprouts

300 g (10½ oz) Greek-style yoghurt

30 ml (1 fl oz) Japanese white soy sauce

500 ml (17 fl oz/2 cups) canola oil

sea salt

30 ml (1 fl oz) hazelnut oil

1 garlic clove, finely chopped

2 thyme sprigs

½ teaspoon freshly ground black pepper

Trim the stalks off the sprouts. Remove the outer dark leaves and set them aside.

Hang the yoghurt in some muslin (cheesecloth) over a bowl for 2–3 hours to thicken it. Discard the whey and mix the curds with the white soy sauce in a bowl. Place in the refrigerator.

Steam the sprouts until just tender and drain well.

Fill a saucepan one-third full with canola oil or put the oil in a deep-fryer and heat it to 170°C (340°F). Fry the brussels sprouts leaves until crisp, then transfer to paper towel to drain. Season lightly with salt and keep warm in a low oven to crisp them.

Heat the hazelnut oil in a frying pan over medium heat, add the brussels sprouts and garlic and sauté until golden. Add the thyme and season with salt and pepper.

To serve, smear some yoghurt over the base of a serving platter and spoon the brussels sprouts over the top. Garnish with the crisp outer leaves.

Using the outer leaves instead of putting them in the bin is a good lesson in parsimony as well as a source of inspiration.

Sauerkraut

— Serves 4–6

Sauerkraut is a very simple preparation and should be a staple of any kitchen and part of any cook's repertoire. Full of probiotics, it is as delicious as it is nutritious, with a lovely acidity and crunch. I love to eat it as is. Traditionally sauerkraut would be cooked with Riesling and several smoked pork products, which is wonderful, but I find its raw state more delicate and versatile. Delicious with grilled meats, steamed fish or barbecued sausages.

1 kg (2 lb 3 oz) white cabbage

20 g (¾ oz) flaked sea salt

Remove and discard the tough outer leaves from the cabbage, then cut the cabbage into quarters.

Using a mandoline, or a very sharp cook's knife, slice the cabbage into 2–3 mm (⅛ in) strips.

Combine the cabbage and salt in a mixing bowl, pressing down a little to release some juice from the cabbage. Transfer to a sealable plastic container or mason jar.

After 24 hours it will begin to bubble. After 48 hours it will produce some gas, which can be vented daily.

Store at room temperature for 5–7 days, turning the container each day, to evenly distribute the juices. After 7 days it should have developed a lovely sour tang and be translucent. Store in the refrigerator.

A spoonful of the fermented juice a day keeps the doctor away.

Left to right: Roast brussels sprouts (page 36); Sauerkraut (page 37).

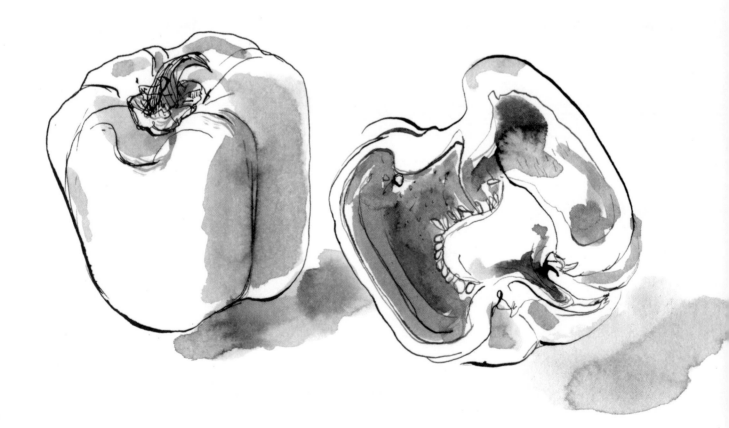

CHAPTER FIVE

—

Capsicum

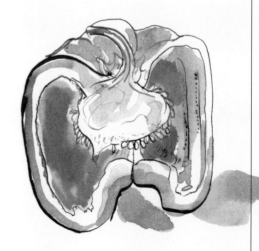

Piperade

— Serves 4

With far more vitamin C than your average orange, the capsicum (bell pepper) is a surprising fruit. Its true character is released by long, slow cooking to reveal a seductive texture and richness. Piperade is the Basque cousin of the more common French ratatouille (with as many versions), and has a delicious affinity with eggs.

---

4 ripe red capsicums (bell peppers)

4 green capsicums (bell peppers)

50 ml (1¾ fl oz) virgin olive oil

1 large red onion, thinly sliced

2 garlic cloves, thinly sliced

1 teaspoon sea salt

4 star anise

1 cinnamon stick

½ teaspoon freshly ground black pepper

10 g (¼ oz) raw (demerara) sugar

4 whole dried chillies

6 ripe tomatoes

Blacken the skin of the capsicums over a gas flame or by using a kitchen blowtorch. When the skins are completely charred, place the capsicums in a container with a tight-fitting lid to steam. When cool, rinse away the skins under running water.

Segment the capsicums following the natural lines, removing the stem and seeds. Pat the segments dry.

Heat 25 ml (¾ fl oz) of the olive oil in a frying pan over medium heat and sauté the onion, garlic, salt and spices until the onion is golden. Transfer to an ovenproof casserole.

Heat the remaining oil in the same frying pan and sauté the capsicum over high heat. Add the sugar and continue to toss until the capsicum starts to caramelise. Transfer this mixture to the casserole along with the dried chillies.

Preheat the oven to 160°C (320°F).

Core the tomatoes and blister the skins with a blowtorch. Gently rub off the skins with paper towel. Chop the tomatoes coarsely and add them to the casserole.

Cover the casserole with a piece of baking paper and bake in the oven for 15–20 minutes until the capsicum is soft. Leave to cool a little then serve.

To make your own dried chillies, buy extra-long red chillies when in season and dehydrate them overnight in a 60°C (140°F) oven. They make an excellent addition to the pantry and can be used wherever you want a deep chilli flavour over the attack of the fresh. Cold-smoke them for amazing complexity (see page 135 for directions).

Harissa

— Makes 500 g (1 lb 2 oz)

Without apology this is one white man's version of the ubiquitous Tunisian staple. It is very versatile and partners happily with most meats, fish and 'Mediterranean' vegetables. Either serve it as a condiment or use it to start or complete an accompanying sauce. You can also use it as a pre-roast rub for whole fish, chicken or roasting cuts. It stores well refrigerated, so make the full amount. (You will thank me later.)

---

1 kg (2 lb 3 oz) red capsicums (bell peppers)

200 g (7 oz) French shallots, sliced

3 long red chillies

100 g (3½ oz) garlic cloves, thinly sliced

100 ml (3½ fl oz) extra-virgin olive oil

1 tablespoon smoked paprika

1 teaspoon ground cumin

1 tablespoon fine salt

Blacken the skin of the capsicums over a gas flame or by using a kitchen blowtorch. When the skins are completely charred, put the capsicums in a container with a tight-fitting lid to steam. When cool, rinse away the skins under running water and pat dry.

Remove the stems and seeds. Cut the capsicums into even-sized pieces.

In a frying pan over low heat, sweat the shallot, chillies and garlic in the olive oil until slightly browned and soft. Stir in the spices and salt. Add the capsicum to the pan and cook until it has softened and most of the liquid has evaporated.

Transfer the mixture to a blender or food processor and process until smooth. Adjust the seasoning to taste.

Store in sterilised jars with a little more oil to cover the surface. Refrigerate for up to 1 month.

⊠

If you want the real thing, Tunisia produces about 22,000 tonnes (tons) of the stuff annually.

Rouille

— Serves 4

Rouille literally means 'rust' and is the traditional accompaniment to the classic fish soups of Marseille. Again, this is an idea based on tradition and something that I've always cooked. I've never been to Marseille, but cooking for me is sometimes illustrating what I imagine a dish would be like. Sometimes I'm disappointed by reality.

---

1 red capsicum (bell pepper)

1 small waxy potato, peeled and cut into thin slices

2 garlic cloves, finely chopped

½ teaspoon dried chilli flakes

1 pinch saffron threads

1 grinding of white pepper

1 teaspoon sea salt

100 ml (3½ fl oz) olive oil

Blacken the skin of the capsicum over a gas flame or by using a kitchen blowtorch. When the skin is completely charred, put the capsicum in a container with a tight-fitting lid to steam. When cool, rinse away the skin under running water and pat dry.

Halve the capsicum, remove the stem and seeds then chop it coarsely.

Put all the ingredients, except the oil, in a small saucepan and cover with water. Cook over medium–low heat until soft and most of the water has reduced.

Transfer the mixture to a blender or food processor and process to a smooth purée, slowly adding the olive oil. Refrigerate and store for up to a week in a sealed container.

Recipes are like opinions, everyone has a different one.

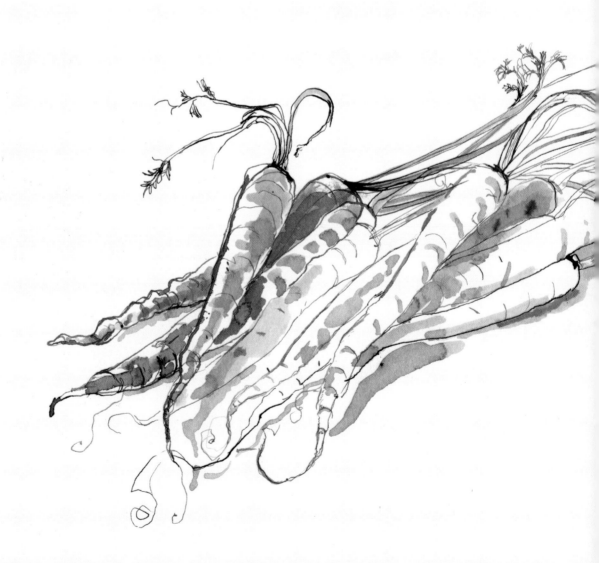

CHAPTER SIX

—

Carrots

Pickled carrots

— Makes 1 kg (2 lb 3 oz)

Pickling is an age-old generic term for preserving and salting and fermentation. Most things are 'pickled' nowadays using some form of heat and vinegar. However, nothing beats the complexity or taste of a naturally fermented product. The indigenous bacteria produce a delightful lactic sourness and also break down the cellular structure of vegetable matter to produce a pleasing crunch without the chew. These pickles can be served as a snack with boiled eggs or as something more substantial with freshly steamed mussels.

---

1 kg (2 lb 3 oz) large carrots, peeled and roots trimmed

40 g (1½ oz) sea salt

3 French shallots

1 teaspoon caraway seeds

1 teaspoon black peppercorns

Cut half the carrots in half lengthways and then into 5 mm (¼ in) slices, or leave them whole if you like. Put them in sterilised mason jars, along with the salt, shallots, caraway seeds and peppercorns.

Juice the remaining carrots and top up the jars with the juice – add water if there is insufficient juice to cover the carrots.

Put the lids on and turn the jars several times and then leave them in a warm, dark place for 1 week. Turn the jars over daily to keep the ferment even and active. Refrigerate for a month or two.

This method works with many different root vegetables. Particularly pleasing results emanated from a bunch of celery.

Confit carrots

— Makes 1 kg (2 lb 3 oz)

'Confit' is a French word meaning to preserve. It usually involves duck, goose or pork and uses some form of fat, cooked long and languidly at low temperature. The fat medium allows the collagen to break down into a gelatinous form without drying the more delicate meat. In the case of the carrot, none of this applies. The long, slow cooking allows the moisture to evaporate, concentrating the flavour compounds and sugars. For most of the cooking, the carrot maintains the horror of boiled carrots past, but persevere and the delicate floral and apricot notes begin to assert themselves and transform this humble vegetable. Serve these as a decadent side dish with fish or meat, on their own, or with home-made vanilla ice cream. There are no rules.

---

1 kg (2 lb 3 oz) large carrots

300 ml (10 fl oz) cold-pressed rice bran oil

1 tablespoon coriander seeds

1 teaspoon white peppercorns

½ lemongrass stem, white part only

Peel the carrots and remove the stems. Cut them in half lengthways and then into 1 cm (½ in) slices. Put them in a heavy-based saucepan with the oil, coriander seeds and peppercorns.

Cut the lemongrass into 5 cm (2 in) pieces, smash with the back of the knife and add them to the saucepan.

Heat to a low simmer and cook for 3–4 hours until the carrots taste like dried apricots. Store them in a sealed jar in their oil until required. These will keep for 2–3 weeks.

To serve, drain the carrots and quickly sauté them – no additional fat required.

Carrot and miso sauce
— *Serves 4*

The cultivated carrot is one of the most important root vegetables grown in temperate regions of the world. Over thousands of years it has transformed from being a small, tough, bitter and spindly root to a fleshy, sweet, pigmented unbranched edible root. For an ostensibly simple vegetable, the carrot does reveal a remarkable versatility for the curious. This recipe also produces excellent results with 'heirloom' varieties. The purple carrot produces a sauce of unsurpassed glossy black inkiness. Experiment with other types of miso for colour, flavour and, most importantly, umami. Excellent with roasted small birds and pink fish.

---

1 kg (2 lb 3 oz) carrots

1 teaspoon red miso paste

½ teaspoon xanthan gum

sea salt

Juice the carrots then pass the juice through a fine sieve. Transfer the juice to a large saucepan and bring to a low simmer over medium heat.

As the carrot juice heats, the carotene will separate and rise to the surface. Skim this off with a kitchen spoon and reserve. Continue skimming the carotene until the juice reduces and starts to clarify. Continue cooking until the juice has reduced to a thin syrup.

Using a hand-held blender, combine the carotene skimmings with the miso paste and carrot syrup. Blend in the xanthan gum to thicken the mixture and season to taste with sea salt. Use within 2–3 days.

Carotene is the orange colour found in carrots and is used, among other things, to colour farmed salmon and bikini-clad oompa loompas.

—

CHAPTER SEVEN

Cheese

Cheese custard

— Serves 4

You can purchase a piece of cheese just for this recipe, but this is something you can do with the remains of cheese plates past. It will work perfectly well with most hard or semi-hard cooked, curd-style cheeses. Parmesan and cheddar have a lovely lactic acidity and concentration, which can handle the addition of the cream and eggs and still retain their composure. Excellent as a cheese course with very ripe pear and salty shortbread.

200 ml (7 fl oz) pouring (single/light) cream

200 g (7 oz) aged cheddar or parmesan, coarsely grated

¼ teaspoon freshly grated nutmeg

¼ teaspoon finely ground white peppercorns

6 eggs

Bring the cream to the boil in a saucepan over medium heat. Add the cheese, nutmeg and pepper, stir to combine and cook until the cheese has melted.

Remove the pan from the heat and blend the mixture well using a hand-held blender.

Crack the eggs into a stainless steel mixing bowl and whisk well. Add the cheese mixture and whisk thoroughly to combine.

Place the bowl over a saucepan of slowly simmering water and cook until the mixture thickens, stirring constantly with a wooden spoon. When thick, remove the bowl from the heat and whisk until tepid. This custard is best consumed at room temperature.

A little technology, such as machines like the Thermomix, make short work of this kind of recipe. If using a Thermomix, set it to 80°C and blend at speed 3–4 for 12–15 minutes until the custard is thick.

Parmesan gnocchi

— Serves 6

Traditionalists would have me flagellated in the town square for calling this gnocchi. Open your minds people, it's just a metaphor for deliciousness.

Kuzu root starch is an exceptional thickener, which can be used like cornflour (cornstarch) or arrowroot, but it is far superior in gelling strength and texture. It is quality starch with a smooth texture, neutral flavour and gives a translucent result. Not only that, it's gluten free! These are a perfect partner for the pumpkin consommé on page 207.

---

450 g (1 lb/4½ cups) grated Parmigiano Reggiano

75 g (2¾ oz) kuzu

5 g (⅛ oz) table salt

Combine the parmesan and 600 ml (20½ fl oz) water in a 1 litre (34 fl oz/4 cup) saucepan and process using a hand-held blender. Cook over medium–low heat until the cheese has melted, then blend with the hand-held blender one more time. Transfer to a container and allow the ingredients to settle in the refrigerator for a minimum of 3 hours or overnight. The broth will separate into a cream on top, liquid in the centre and solids on the bottom.

Carefully pour the parmesan cream and liquid into a saucepan. Discard the remaining solids.

Whisk the kuzu and salt into the parmesan liquid over high heat until thick and elastic.

Allow to cool slightly then transfer to a piping (icing) bag fitted with a 1 cm (½ in) nozzle. While still hot, quickly pipe the mixture into an ice bath in 30 cm (12 in) lengths.

After 30 minutes, remove the parmesan gnocchi from the water and drain on a perforated tray. Cut into 2 cm (¾ in) lengths and place on a tray lined with plastic wrap. The gnocchi can be kept for 1 day in the refrigerator. They can be served at room temperature or just warm them in a low (50°C/120°F) oven for 5 minutes. Serve in a delicate broth or on top of a fine tomato sauce

For the well-heeled and equipped, combine the parmesan and water in a Thermomix. Cook at speed 5 for 10 minutes at 80°C, until the cheese and water emulsify to a broth. This replaces step 1.

Ricotta dumplings

— Serves 6

This delicious recipe comes courtesy of my very talented chef and partner in Pei Modern, Matt Germanchis. The delicate texture of the ricotta is well served here and doesn't require too much garnish. This is an excellent base recipe, which can adapt to the vagaries of the season, so do vary it according to the produce at hand. Spring peas, young spinach, a sauce of fresh tomato and tarragon, tiny flowering zucchini (courgettes), lemon thyme. I could go on.

900 g (2 lb) fresh ricotta

3 egg yolks

fresh nutmeg

1 teaspoon salt

½ teaspoon freshly ground white pepper

185 g (6½ oz/1¼ cups) plain (all-purpose) flour

olive oil for shallow-frying

Hang the ricotta in a piece of muslin (cheesecloth) for 3 hours to separate the curds from the whey. Discard the whey and put the ricotta curds in a large mixing bowl.

Whisk the egg yolks with a good grating of nutmeg and the salt and pepper.

Put the egg mixture in the bowl with the ricotta and stir to combine. Sift the flour over the ricotta mixture, then use your hands to knead briefly until you form a soft dough. If the mixture is still sticky, add a little more flour.

Turn the dough out onto a lightly floured work surface and cut it into four equal-sized pieces.

Using your hands, gently roll each piece out to form a log about 2 cm (¾ in) in diameter. With a lightly floured knife, cut each log into 1.5 cm (½ in) long pieces.

To serve, bring a large saucepan of salted water to the boil. Add about eight dumplings per person and cook in simmering water for 2 minutes or until they float to the surface. Prepare your garnish separately and combine on the serving plate as the dumplings are a little delicate.

If you make our butter recipe on page 103, the whey will produce an amount of excellent ricotta.

CHAPTER EIGHT

—

Chicken

Roast chicken

— Serves 4

This is my go-to dish for any occasion, prompt or informal. It relies on the quality of the bird, so buy the best you can afford. Rubbing the skin with oil ensures it will be crisp and gives something for the salt and spices to adhere to. The chilli adds a certain frisson and shouldn't be omitted.

---

1 × 1.8 kg (4 lb) free-range chicken

½ bunch of thyme

25 ml (¾ fl oz) virgin olive oil

1 teaspoon dried chilli flakes

1 teaspoon sea salt flakes

freshly ground white pepper

1 lemon

1 red onion

2 teaspoons cornflour (cornstarch)

Preheat the oven to 180°C (350°F).

Rinse the chicken under cool running water and pat dry with paper towel.

Spread the thyme over the base of a roasting tin and put the chicken on top. Rub the chicken with the olive oil, ensuring it is thoroughly covered. Sprinkle over the chilli, salt and a good grinding of white pepper.

Cut the lemon and onion into quarters and add them to the tin. Roast for 1½ hours, with the cavity of the chicken facing the rear of the oven. To test if the chicken is cooked through, look at the juices in the cavity. They should just be turning brown. If they are still bloody, another 5 minutes or so should suffice.

When the chicken is ready, remove it from the roasting tin and put it on a warm plate to rest.

Put the roasting tin on the stove top and remove some of the fat. Turn the heat to high and add 250 ml (8½ fl oz/1 cup) water. Bring to the boil, scraping the tin to incorporate the caramelised pan juices. Pass the jus through a fine sieve into a small saucepan.

In a cup or small bowl, make a slurry with the cornflour and 1 tablespoon cold water and then whisk this mixture into the jus. Whisk over medium heat until thickened slightly.

Carve the chicken and squeeze over the roast lemon quarters. Serve with the jus.

I always serve this chicken with roast potatoes. I use desirée for preference but any waxy variety is fine. Peel the potatoes and cut them into eighths. Soak in cold water for a few minutes. Drain and then microwave on High (100%) for 2–3 minutes in a sealed container to set the starch and prevent them from sticking. Heat a heavy, cast-iron roasting tin in the oven. When hot, add 80 ml (2½ fl oz/⅓ cup) olive oil. Drain the potatoes again and rub them dry in a clean tea towel (dish towel). Place them in the tin in an orderly fashion. They should sizzle. Brush them with some of the oil in the tin and season well with sea salt flakes. They will be done when the chicken is ready. Don't be tempted to turn them until this time and you will be rewarded with a glassy, golden crunch.

Poached chicken with rice
— Serves 4–6

I first ate this Hainanese classic in the hawker stalls of Singapore. I have eaten it many times since and cook it mostly during Sydney's humid summers. Some may find the gelatinous texture of the meat and skin a little rich. Others fear death from salmonella when they see the pink blush around the bone. I have no time for these people.

1 × 1.6 kg (3½ lb) free-range chicken

100 ml (3½ fl oz) light soy sauce

3 cm (1¼ in) piece fresh ginger

2 fresh bay leaves

1 bunch of coriander (cilantro), plus extra to garnish

1 baby cucumber, halved lengthways, or thinly sliced red onion, to garnish

DRESSING

1 tablespoon first-pressing sesame oil

1 tablespoon soy sauce

CHICKEN RICE

reserved chicken fat (see method)

440 g (15½ oz/2 cups) short- or medium-grain white rice

625 ml (21 fl oz/2½ cups) chicken stock

2 cm (¾ in) piece fresh ginger, finely chopped

Fill a 4 litre (135 fl oz/16 cup) saucepan three-quarters full with water and bring it to the boil. Add the chicken and cook for 1 minute. Drain and refresh the chicken under cool water.

Rinse and clean the saucepan and add the chicken and the remaining ingredients, except the garnish. Add water to cover and cook over high heat until it comes to a simmer. Skim to remove any scum. Cook for 5 minutes then remove the pan from the heat, cover with a tight-fitting lid and leave for 2 hours. Once it has finished cooking, skim off 125 ml (4 fl oz/½ cup) of the chicken fat and reserve. (See note.)

To make the dressing, combine the sesame oil and soy sauce in a small bowl.

To make the chicken rice, put the reserved chicken fat in a 1 litre (34 fl oz/4 cup) saucepan, add the rice and cook over medium heat until the rice just starts to toast. Add the stock and bring to the boil. Add the ginger and cover the pan with a tight-fitting lid. Reduce the heat to a low simmer and cook for 12–15 minutes. Remove the pan from the heat and fluff the rice with a fork. Replace the lid and allow the rice to steam, off the heat, for another 15 minutes.

Remove the chicken from the saucepan and cut it into 12 pieces, Chinese-style, leaving it on the bone. Serve the chicken at room temperature with the dressing drizzled over accompanied by the chicken rice. Garnish with the extra coriander and the baby cucumber.

You can freeze the leftover stock and use it as the base for a master stock whenever you cook this dish.

Casarecce reggiano
with chicken dumplings

— Serves 4

I first learnt the technique of cooking pasta in its own sauce from reading Alain Ducasse, a native Niçois. I subsequently learnt that it was a common technique across southern Italy and not restricted to the French city of Nice. Cultures blur along borders and this dish, while tipping its hat to the border city, has a Jewish influence with the chicken dumplings, and I think a little Greek with the addition of lemon juice. This dish has always been on the menu at Pei Modern and all we ask is a little patience while we prepare it to order.

---

80 ml (2½ fl oz/⅓ cup) olive oil

100 g (3½ oz) butter

300 g (10½ oz) casarecce

700 ml (23½ fl oz) chicken stock

150 g (5½ oz/1½ cups) Parmigiano Reggiano

juice of ½ lemon

white pepper

CONFIT GIZZARDS

100 g (3½ oz) chicken gizzards

150 ml (5 fl oz) duck fat

CHICKEN DUMPLINGS

600 g (1 lb 5 oz) boneless, skinless chicken breast

4 chicken livers

10 chicken hearts

180 ml (6 fl oz) pouring (single/light) cream

½ nutmeg

½ teaspoon white pepper

We like Benedetto Cavalieri casarecce, or any hard durum wheat product, or use good-quality rigatoni or penne instead. The starch from the pasta thickens the sauce as it reduces and makes it incredibly rich, so watch the salt levels.

To make the confit gizzards, put the gizzards and duck fat in a heavy-based saucepan over low heat and simmer for 2 hours or until tender. Drain and cool then chop the gizzards coarsely.

To make the chicken dumplings, use a kitchen knife to separately chop the chicken breast, livers and hearts into a coarse mince.

Transfer half the chopped breast to a food processor and process until quite fine. Add the cream in a thin stream and continue to process to form a mousse. Add the chicken heart, liver, gizzards and remaining chicken breast, nutmeg, 1 teaspoon salt and the white pepper to the food processor and pulse to combine.

Cook a small spoonful in simmering water until firm to test for balance of flavour and texture. Adjust the seasoning to taste.

To make the casarecce, put the olive oil and 40 g (1½ oz) of the butter in a heavy-based saucepan over low heat. Add the pasta and stir to coat it evenly. Add the chicken stock and cook for 10 minutes, stirring constantly.

Using a dessertspoon, make small balls of the chicken dumpling mixture and add it to the pasta (approximately 3–4 balls per person). Cook for a further 10 minutes.

Remove the pan from the heat and finish with the Parmigiano Reggiano and the remaining butter. Finish with a squeeze of lemon juice and a generous grinding of white pepper.

—

CHAPTER NINE

Chocolate

Chocolate tart

— *Makes 2 tarts*

This is based on one of the great tarts in the tart lexicon and originates from his eminence, Chef Joël Robuchon. It is a lesson in simplicity and elegance. The chocolate does the heavy lifting in texture and flavour. It should only be eaten freshly prepared, for its lustre is tarnished by time and refrigeration. I have changed the traditional pastry to a very short chocolate crust. Why? Because I think it's better.

TART SHELL

150 g (5½ oz) butter, softened

75 g (2¾ oz) caster (superfine) sugar

½ teaspoon salt

125 g (4½ oz) plain (all-purpose) flour

50 g (1¾ oz) rice flour

50 g (1¾ oz) unsweetened (Dutch) cocoa powder

1 egg, lightly beaten

FILLING

200 g (7 oz) best-quality chocolate (72% cocoa solids)

190 ml (6½ fl oz/¾ cup) pouring (single/light) cream

80 ml (2½ fl oz/⅓ cup) milk

1 egg, lightly beaten

To make the tart shells, put the butter and sugar in the bowl of a stand mixer fitted with the paddle attachment and beat until pale and creamy.

In a bowl, sift together the salt, flours and cocoa powder.

Using a spatula, fold the flours into the butter mixture until just coming together. Do not mix them using the electric mixer or you will overwork the dough and the tart base will shrink.

Tip the rough contents onto a work surface and, using the heel of your hand, press down and away from you to spread the dough. Repeat three times.

Scrape the dough together and divide it into two balls. Flatten each ball slightly and wrap individually with plastic wrap. Refrigerate for 30 minutes.

Roll one ball of dough into a circle about 5 mm (¼ in) thick. Place a 22 cm (8¾ in) tart ring on the dough and run the tip of a knife around the inside of the ring. Remove any excess dough. Remove the tart ring. Repeat with the second ball of dough.

Place the tart bases on a baking tray and refrigerate for another 30 minutes.

Preheat the oven to 160°C (320°F).

Bake the tart bases in the oven for 10–12 minutes until the dough is dry. It will firm up once it cools.

Lightly beat the egg and use a pastry brush to paint a thin layer across the cooled bases. Return to the oven for 3 minutes to set the egg. This will prevent the base from going soggy once the filling is added.

To make the filling, coarsely chop the chocolate and place it in a medium heatproof bowl.

Bring the cream and milk to the boil in a small saucepan. Pour the hot milk mixture over the chocolate and stir until melted. Whisk in the egg until fully incorporated.

Reduce the oven temperature to 100°C (210°F).

Place the two tart rings back over the baked bases. Pour the filling evenly between the two rings. Bake for 8–10 minutes until the filling is just set. It should still have a slight jiggle. Leave to firm at room temperature for 1 hour.

Serve at room temperature within 2–3 hours. Do not refrigerate or the tart filling will lose its texture.

Dried chocolate mousse

— Serves 4 or 1

This is just a classic chocolate mousse recipe in a different form. Feel free to stop there if you please. In a world where too much chocolate is barely enough, I can visualise serving this chocolatey magnificence with a freshly made chocolate mousse, a bowl of whipped vanilla cream and a small mountain of raspberries. I can't imagine anything could be wrong in such a world.

---

300 g (10½ oz) best-quality dark chocolate (72% cocoa solids)

5 egg yolks

100 g (3½ oz) caster (superfine) sugar

400 g (14 oz) egg whites

In a heatproof bowl set over a saucepan of simmering water, melt the chocolate. Do not let the water touch the base of the bowl and do not heat above 50°C (122°F). Set aside to cool slightly.

In a separate bowl, whisk the egg yolks and half the sugar until light and fluffy. Pour the chocolate mixture into the egg mixture and stir slowly to combine.

In another bowl, whisk the remaining sugar and the egg whites to soft peaks. Use a spatula to carefully fold them into the chocolate mixture, in three batches.

Spread the mixture onto non-stick ovenproof mats, to a thickness of about 1 cm (½ in). Dry in an oven overnight at 70°C (160°F) to crisp. Store in an airtight container for up to 3 days.

Such a simple delight rests on the quality of its ingredients. Buy the best chocolate you can and keep it above 70% cocoa solids if we are to remain friends.

Chocolate jelly

— Serves 4

Two words: jelly, chocolate.

This is lovely to set in a classic jelly mould. I would accompany it with blood orange segments and whipped vanilla cream. It wouldn't complain if partnered with poached pears, quinces or vanilla custard.

Neither would I.

---

14 g (½ oz) gelatine leaves

140 g (5 oz) caster (superfine) sugar

160 g (5½ oz) dark crème de cacao

40 g (1½ oz/⅓ cup) dark, unsweetened (Dutch) cocoa powder

Soak the gelatine leaves in iced water until very soft.

Bring the sugar, 750 ml (25½ fl oz/3 cups) water, the crème de cacao and cocoa powder to the boil in a saucepan over medium heat.

Squeeze the excess water from the gelatine leaves and whisk them into the chocolate mix until the gelatine has dissolved. Pass the mixture through a fine sieve into a jelly mould and place in the refrigerator to set, about 2–3 hours.

To serve, quickly dip the mould in hot water and turn the jelly out onto a lovely antique plate.

CHAPTER TEN

Citrus

Orange and polenta cake
— *Serves 4*

Google pulled up 1,240,000 results for this cake in 22 seconds. I'm not sure when it became a thing but who knows what is going to go viral these days. The cake recipe is as sound as it is common and I've cooked it for 25 years. My version adds a kick with the syrup and Chartreuse chaser. Serve with Crème fraîche (page 103) or natural yoghurt.

---

2 small oranges

butter for greasing

flour for dusting

5 large eggs (55–60 g/2 oz)

170 g (6 oz/¾ cup) caster (superfine) sugar

170 g (6 oz/1⅔ cups) ground almonds

50 g (1¾ oz/⅓ cup) polenta

1 teaspoon baking powder

SYRUP

1 vanilla bean

230 g (8 oz/1 cup) caster (superfine) sugar

4 cardamom pods

2 star anise

50 ml (1¾ fl oz) Chartreuse

To make the syrup, split the vanilla bean and scrape the seeds into a small saucepan over medium–low heat – throw in the pod as well. Add the sugar, 250 ml (8½ fl oz/1 cup) water and the remaining spices. Bring to a gentle simmer, cook for 5 minutes then remove the pan from the heat. Add the Chartreuse and allow to infuse for 30 minutes. Strain into a clean container.

Put the oranges, unpeeled, in a saucepan, cover with water and bring to the boil over medium–high heat. Reduce the heat to medium–low, cover and simmer for 1¼ hours until the oranges are very soft. Drain and cool for 30 minutes.

Preheat the oven to 190°C (375°F).

Butter a 24 cm (9½ in) springform cake tin and line the base with a disc of baking paper. Butter the tin again, including the paper, and lightly dust with flour – shake out any excess.

Coarsely chop the boiled oranges, removing any pips, then transfer them to a food processor and purée.

Whisk together the eggs and sugar for 2 minutes. Stir in the ground almonds and polenta and sift in the baking powder. Add the puréed oranges and mix well. Pour the mixture into the tin and bake for 40–45 minutes until light golden and just firm to the touch. Leave to cool in the tin for 10 minutes, then turn out onto a wire rack to cool.

Transfer the cake to a serving plate and use a skewer to prick it all over. Spoon over some of the syrup and allow it to soak in before adding more. Continue until all the syrup has been used.

Any citrus fruit is suitable, but obviously make sure to maintain a similar weight. Two mandarins will a dry cake make.

Mandarin sherbet

— Serves 4

Before the internet, kids had fireworks night, a long walk home from school and sherbet. The liquorice straw in the sherbet gave out with the first suck but continued to give good service as a dipping stick. It wasn't a sharing thing. We also had Wizz Fizz (popping candy) with tiny plastic spoons and a little plastic ring that would only fit a monkey.

This version can be given an AO rating by simply using the skin of a grapefruit instead. Kids and the dull of mind do not like bitter. Amazing with chocolate or vanilla ice cream.

---

4 mandarins

95 g (3¼ oz) icing (confectioners') sugar

3 g (¹⁄₁₀ oz) citric acid

3 g (¹⁄₁₀ oz) tartaric acid

Peel the mandarins and reserve the flesh for another use. Put the peel on a baking tray and cook overnight in a 55–60°C (130–140°F) oven to dry and crisp.

Put the dry mandarin peel in a spice grinder and blend to a very fine powder. Add it to the remaining ingredients in a bowl and combine. Pass the mixture through a fine sieve. Store in an airtight container.

Add 3 g (¹⁄₁₀ oz) bicarbonate of soda (baking soda) for fizz and serve with a frozen citrus curd (see page 87) to match.

Frozen orange curd

— Serves 10–12

Let's start with orange, but also consider grapefruit (ruby and golden), mandarin and lemons (Meyer and lemonade). All will do very well with this basic curd recipe. Again, for those who wish to, or who have no freezing device, it would be perfectly acceptable and delicious to stop at the curd. For those who don't and do, frozen Nirvana awaits.

---

500 ml (17 fl oz/2 cups) orange juice

55 ml (1¾ fl oz) lemon juice

395 g (14 oz) caster (superfine) sugar

18 eggs

350 g (12½ oz) cold butter, diced

Put the orange juice, lemon juice, sugar and eggs in a heatproof bowl and whisk to combine.

Put the bowl over a saucepan of simmering water and whisk constantly until the mixture reaches 80°C (176°F). Remove the bowl from the heat and slowly add the butter, allowing each piece to be fully incorporated before adding the next.

When the ingredients are combined, pass the curd through a fine sieve. Place in the refrigerator until cold.

Churn in an ice cream machine according to the manufacturer's instructions.

Nothing else required, except a spoon – and beware brain freeze.

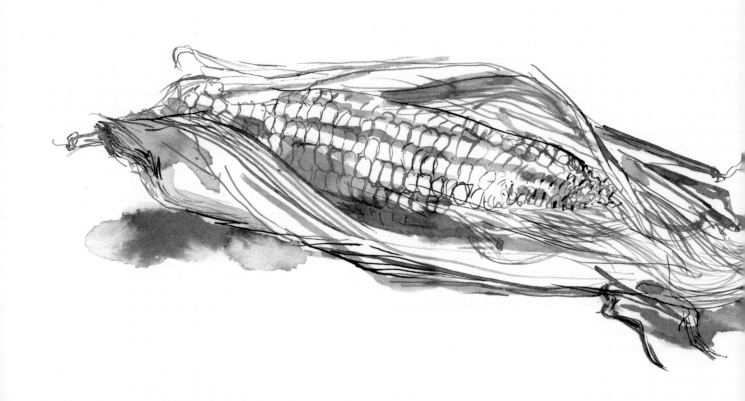

CHAPTER ELEVEN

—

Corn

Baked corn

— Serves 4

I loved Warner Brothers 'Looney Tunes' cartoons as a kid. They were highly influential on a young, silly mind, especially when it came to eating corn. There was the 'buzzsaw' method, where you would rotate the corn, eating as fast as possible, or 'the typewriter', eating two rows at a time from left to right, then 'ding' and back. We had little 'corn forks' – two prongs on each and the handle a mini plastic corn. A good, fast boil, a smear of margarine and that interminable time it took the temperature to abate so that your teeth didn't feel like they were boiling in your gums.

---

80 g (2¾ oz) butter, at room temperature

½ teaspoon freshly ground black pepper

½ teaspoon dried chilli flakes

1 teaspoon sea salt flakes

4 corn cobs

2 kaffir limes

Preheat the oven to 180°C (350°F).

In a bowl, mix the butter, pepper, chilli and salt.

Peel back the husks of the corn and remove and discard the silks.

Spread the butter mixture evenly over each cob, then pull the husks back into place. Roll each cob in a square of baking paper. Twist each end and tie with butcher's string. Bake for 30 minutes.

Serve the corn cobs in their paper, with each diner unravelling their own parcel and squeezing over half a kaffir lime.

If you have a square metre of dirt under the sun, grow your own corn.

Fermented corn

— Makes 2 cups

Sweet corn in its natural form is not particularly nutritious. High in fibre, it is full of simple glucose and sucrose. Lord knows the kids get enough of that. Fermentation breaks down the cell structure to make it more digestible, with the added kick of probiotics. This basic process and salt ratio can be applied to many ingredients and I've nary come across one that wasn't improved in texture and flavour. Use this as it is with fish or white or smoked meats. Or use it as the base for a salsa or, even better, with guacamole, corn (taco) chips and a beer.

---

4 corn cobs

2% salt to the total weight of corn

Use a sharp knife to remove the kernels from the cobs – do not cut too close to the cob as the corn will become bitter.

Weigh the corn kernels and add 2% of its weight in salt. Mix well and tip into a large resealable sandwich bag. Remove all the air and seal. Place in a warm spot for 5–7 days. Turn the bag over daily to maintain an even ferment.

When ready, the corn will be slightly acidic. Store it in the bag or transfer to a sealed jar, refrigerated, for up to a week.

Corn custard

— Makes 250 g (9 oz/1 cup)

This fairly simple preparation was actually somewhat of a revelation – the fact that the corn could be transformed using nothing more than the starch it contained. It was the purity and simplicity of this concept that still gets me excited. This makes an unsurpassed partner for pink fish. Think smoked trout.

5 corn cobs

½ teaspoon sea salt

Peel the husks and remove the silks. Use a sharp knife to cut the kernels from the cobs – avoid cutting too close to the cob or the custard will turn bitter.

Transfer the kernels to a food processor and blend them to a purée. Pass the mixture through a fine sieve, using the back of a ladle to press down on the solids.

Put the corn juice in a saucepan over medium–low heat and simmer, whisking constantly, until the juice thickens. After 10 minutes or so, the starch in the corn will bloom and thicken the mixture.

Remove the pan from the heat and cool it down in an ice bath.

Whisk until smooth and season to taste. Store in the refrigerator for a day or two.

Chop the naked cobs and bake in a medium (170–180°C/340–350°F) oven until golden. Cover with water in a small saucepan and simmer for 1 hour to make a golden corn stock. Add gelatine to set it into a wobbly, savoury jelly.

CHAPTER TWELVE

–

Cream

Crème anglaise

— Serves 4–6

Crème anglaise, English cream, vanilla custard. Who cares what it's called and who stole it from whom. The fact is, it was one of the better things to come from that long-standing enmity. It is drinkable in this form but let me say that whoever decided to freeze it, is surely being rewarded by a state of Nirvana.

Serve with stewed fruit or with (very) thinly sliced banana and a sprinkling of instant coffee.

---

500 ml (17 fl oz/2 cups) full-cream (whole) milk

2 vanilla beans, split and seeds scraped

120 g (4½ oz) caster (superfine) sugar

180 g (6½ oz) egg yolks

Put the milk, split vanilla beans and their seeds and half the sugar in a saucepan over medium heat.

Put the egg yolks in a large bowl and whisk in the remaining sugar until pale and a light mousse forms.

When the milk starts to rise in the pan, whisk it into the eggs in a thin stream to avoid curdling the eggs. Whisk well and then return to the pan. Cook over low heat, stirring with a wooden spoon until it thickens (just on 80°C/176°F for the technical). A finger dragged across the back of the spoon will leave its mark. When this holds, the custard is ready.

Pour the custard through a sieve into a clean bowl set over an ice bath and whisk from time to time to cool and prevent splitting.

If the custard splits, do not persevere. There is no remedy worth eating. Give yourself a light slap and start again with fresh ingredients.

Sauternes custard

— Makes 6–8

This little custard has been on the menu at Marque since the beginning and, as clever as I think I am, people keep asking for this one thing above all others. The curse of the signature dish. You, dear reader, really should master it at home.

---

375 ml (12½ fl oz/1½ cups) Sauternes-style sweet wine (around 110 g per litre/15 oz per gallon residual sugar)

120 g (4½ oz) caster (superfine) sugar

3 whole eggs, plus 9 egg yolks

700 ml (23½ fl oz) pouring (single/light) cream

BITTER CARAMEL

250 g (9 oz) sugar

Preheat the oven to 100°C (210°F).

Bring the Sauternes and caster sugar to the boil in a saucepan over medium heat.

In a bowl, whisk together the eggs and egg yolks. Pour the Sauternes mixture over the eggs, whisking all the time. Whisk in the cream. Pass the mixture through a fine sieve and skim any bubbles.

Pour the custard into ramekins and kiss with the flame of a kitchen blowtorch to remove any remaining bubbles.

Bake in a bain-marie (water bath) for approximately 40 minutes or until just set.

To make the bitter caramel, heat a small, heavy-based saucepan over medium heat. Add the sugar and stir with a wooden spoon to avoid the caramel burning. Once the sugar has melted and reached a dark caramel colour, remove the pan from the heat. Pour in 110 ml (4 fl oz) water carefully, as it will bubble and spit. Allow to cool.

To serve, pour a thin layer of caramel over the custards and serve immediately.

If you want to be clever, purchase a French, spring-loaded egg topper and bake the custards in egg shells. Use the egg carton to hold them during baking.

Crème fraîche and freshly churned butter

— *Makes 3 litres (101 fl oz/12 cups) crème fraîche*

There is almost nothing more satisfying than making your own crème fraîche, or cultured cream. The transformation is wondrous. I've made it in such a quantity because a large measure should be eaten as is, with the remainder churned for butter. The by-products of buttermilk and whey are worth the effort alone.

Most commercial butters have a level of rancidity through oxidisation. The difference is revealing.

0.1 g butter culture (Danisco MM100) (available from Amazon, so not hard to get)

3 litres (101 fl oz/12 cups) organic pouring (single/light) cream (35–40% milk fat)

Put the butter culture in a small bowl and set aside.

In a large saucepan over low heat, bring the cream to 25°C (77°F).

Take a small ladleful of cream and add it to the butter culture. Whisk thoroughly to create the starter slurry.

Continue heating the remainder of the cream to 37.5°C (99.5°F). Immediately pour it into a clean, sterilised bucket or other large container, and add the starter slurry. Whisk together to evenly disperse. Cover the bucket with a clean tea towel (dish towel) and leave at room temperature (above 20°C/68°F) for 12–15 hours. It will look quite thick after this time.

Refrigerate and use after 2–3 days, depending on the level of sourness you prefer.

Cream is best cultured near its expiry date and best churned 2 weeks after culturing.

BUTTER

Using a whisk attachment, churn some crème fraîche in the bowl of a stand mixer on medium speed until it splits and the butter fat resembles popcorn.

Strain through a colander and capture the buttermilk.

Rinse the butter under cold running water to remove any excess buttermilk. Strain the remaining buttermilk through a fine sieve and reserve for another use.

Put the butterfat back in the bowl of the mixer fitted with the paddle attachment, and mix on low speed to separate any remaining water. Drain the water as required. When no water remains, the butter is ready to be moulded.

Cut it into even portions and wrap it in baking paper. Refrigerate and use as required. It is best used within 7–10 days.

Before starting, have all the equipment sterilised and ready. Use a proprietary product, such as Milton sterilising tablets or liquids used for babies' bottles. Make sure you use the lactic culture specified for its flavour profile. Don't use a yoghurt culture as it makes the cream and resulting butter smell unpleasantly cheesy.

CHAPTER THIRTEEN

—

Duck

Duck ham

— Serves 4

This is entry-level charcuterie and is perfect for the domestic kitchen. There is almost nothing that doesn't benefit from curing and drying through evaporation, including duck breast. Duck is particularly pleasing as a ham due to its natural red flesh and creamy white fat. To slice it transparently, melt-on-the-tongue thin, partially freeze it to slice with a razor-sharp knife or rotary slicer. Serve with fresh figs for true beauty.

---

1 cinnamon stick

2 allspice berries

3 cloves

2 star anise

5 white peppercorns

500 g (1 lb 2 oz) coarse salt

250 g (9 oz) raw (demerara) sugar

4 boneless duck breasts

Toast the spices in a dry frying pan over high heat, until they begin to pop and become aromatic. Transfer to a spice grinder, or use a mortar and pestle, and grind to a fine powder.

In a bowl, combine the salt, sugar and ground spices.

Trim the duck breast of any fatty flaps.

Fill a deep container with half the salt mixture. Put the duck breasts on top and cover with the remaining salt mixture. Ensure the breasts are completely covered. Leave in the refrigerator for 5 days.

Remove the duck breasts from the curing mixture, rinse under cool running water and pat dry. Wrap in muslin (cheesecloth) and store in the refrigerator for a week or two prior to using – hang from a shelf for best results. Slice thinly before serving, if desired.

Cold-smoke anything to go to flavour town. Prior to hanging, follow the instructions for smoking on page 135.

Confit duck

— Serves 4

Confit is a french culinary term meaning to cook and prove in oil. While it is now served wherever the French are appreciated, it originated and is emblematic of the Gascony region in the South West. The same technique can be used for a goose (if you are so fortunate) and secondary cuts of pork. On that note: this technique is perfect for relaxing a tougher cut, which is why it's used for legs and shoulders.

2 teaspoons white peppercorns

2 teaspoons coriander seeds

1 bunch of thyme, leaves picked

4 bay leaves

2 teaspoons juniper berries

1 garlic bulb

2 oranges

105 g (3½ oz/⅓ cup) coarse sea salt

8 free-range duck leg quarters (marylands), French-trimmed

1 kg (2 lb 3 oz) duck fat

In a bowl, combine the peppercorns, coriander seeds, thyme, bay leaves and juniper berries.

Crush the garlic bulb, remove the stem and add it to the spices.

Peel the oranges and use a small, sharp knife to remove the pith. Add them to the spices.

Transfer the mixture to a food processor and process to a fine paste. Add the salt and pulse to combine.

Rub a good amount of the spice mixture into the flesh side of the duck leg quarters, then place them on a plastic tray. Sprinkle over the remainder of the spice mixture and refrigerate overnight.

The following day, drain the liquid and rub away any remaining salt crystals using paper towel.

Heat the duck fat in a large casserole to 90°C (194°F). Add the duck and maintain at this temperature for 1½–2 hours until the thigh bone starts to loosen from the flesh. Remove from the heat to cool.

The duck can be eaten immediately, but it is far better when left to cure for 2–3 months. To do this, place the legs in layers in a non-reactive container – a wide-mouthed mason jar is perfect. Pour over the cooking fat to cover and knock the jar to remove any air bubbles. Make sure the fat covers the flesh by 2–3 cm (¾–1¼ in). Refrigerated, this will last for 6 months.

The true gift of this recipe is the fat. Fry slices of waxy potatoes in it and serve with a chicory (endive) salad to be deliciously traditional.

Super-crispy roast duck
— Serves 4

I once went to Beijing to cook and, not being particularly sharp and the recipient of a simple country education, it took me a while to remember that the city was formerly named Peking. A little while later the penny dropped and I thought this was probably the home of Peking duck and that was why it was served with wheat pancakes, as it is in the North. The only version I had eaten was in Cantonese restaurants – definitely rice territory. All of this took some time. One of the finest was had at Da Dong. Chef Dong Zhenxiang roasts his in brick ovens fuelled by fruit wood, including persimmon.

The duck is properly served with a sweet tian mian jiang dipping sauce, made from fermented soybeans – not hoisin plum, which is a corruption.

---

1 × 1.8 kg (4 lb) free-range duck

1 teaspoon juniper berries

1 teaspoon allspice

1 teaspoon Sichuan pepper

1 teaspoon white peppercorns

1 teaspoon coriander seeds

20 g (¾ oz) sea salt flakes

2 mandarins

125 g (4½ oz) fine salt

100 ml (3½ fl oz) sherry vinegar

Rinse the duck under cold running water and pat dry with paper towel.

Grind the spices with the sea salt flakes using a mortar and pestle.

Blend the whole mandarins in a food processor and add the spices.

Spread the spiced mandarin paste evenly into the cavity of the duck. Seal the cavity with a stainless steel skewer.

Bring 3 litres (101 fl oz/12 cups) water and the fine salt to the boil and add the vinegar. Roll the duck in the water to tighten and set the skin, then place the duck on a wire rack to cool. Refrigerate for 2 days, uncovered, to dry the skin.

Preheat the oven to 200°C (400°F).

Place the duck on a wire rack in a deep roasting tin. Cook in the oven for 25 minutes. Reduce the heat to 160°C (320°F) and cook for a further 45 minutes. Remove the duck from the oven and rest it for 15 minutes before serving. Remove the skewer and drain the juices and fat from the cavity. Discard. The fat from the cooking tray can be retained.

MARK BEST / BEST KITCHEN BASICS

CHAPTER FOURTEEN

Egg

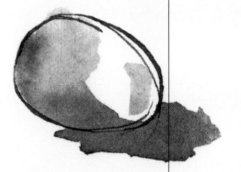

Perfectly boiled eggs

— Serves 4–6

I think I'm quite alone in that I don't particularly like ramen. Maybe that's an exaggeration. I don't mind it, but wouldn't queue for it. I probably can't be bothered to queue for anything, to be honest. If I have ramen, I eat it quietly, which evidently is completely missing the point. The proper way is to slurp the noodles, pulling in lots of air at the same time. Frankly I would have received a slap on the head for those table manners when I was young. You don't forget those lessons.

The best bit for me are the perfectly cooked eggs – easily peeled with a custardy, brilliantly coloured yolk centred in a firm white. They are a revelation against the sulphurous green–grey of the overcooked, hard-boiled egg. I've included a ramen egg marinade, because it tastes quite good.

---

6 free-range eggs, at room temperature

RAMEN MARINADE

125 ml (4 fl oz/½ cup) sake

125 ml (4 fl oz/½ cup) light soy sauce

125 ml (4 fl oz/½ cup) mirin

1 cm (½ in) piece fresh ginger, thinly sliced

To make the ramen marinade, in a small saucepan over medium–low heat, combine the sake, soy sauce, mirin and ginger and bring to a low simmer. Remove the pan from the heat and allow to infuse for 10 minutes.

Choose a pan in which you will be able to fit the eggs in one layer. Add enough water to just cover the eggs.

Prick each egg with a needle, on the wider end, to allow any air to escape.

Bring the water to a low simmer then carefully add the eggs – use a spoon so they won't hit the bottom and crack. Cook for exactly 6 minutes, stirring the eggs gently every 30 seconds to centre the yolk. Remove the eggs and immediately put them in an ice bath to stop the cooking. Leave for 10 minutes then peel.

Put the eggs in the marinade, cover with plastic wrap and leave overnight to give a lovely golden brown colour.

You don't have to use the marinade. Just cook the eggs this way whenever a good boiled egg is required.

Cured egg yolks
— *Makes 12*

A happy clutch of chickens can produce a lot of eggs. Again, preserving comes to the fore – not just to prolong the bounty of the season but to create something unique and allow many further applications of a base product. Use a microplane to grate these eggs over green vegetables, steamed vegetables or salad to add a hit of umami.

---

700 g (1 lb 9 oz) salt

300 g (10½ oz) sugar

12 free-range egg yolks

Combine the salt and sugar in a bowl.

Take a deep tray and half-fill it with the salt and sugar mixture and smooth the surface.

Using an egg shell, create 12 indentations in the salt.

Carefully place each yolk in an indentation and cover with the remaining cure mix. Tightly wrap the tray in plastic wrap and refrigerate.

The yolks will take approximately 7 days to cure. They are ready when they are firm and translucent.

Remove the eggs from the cure mixture and gently rinse off any remaining mixture under cold running water. Store in an airtight container in the refrigerator.

A delicious variation is to cure the yolks in miso with a dash of sake. The eggs take on the cure flavour very well. Another variation is to make egg yolk noodles. Place the cured egg yolks on a piece of baking paper 1 cm (½ in) apart. Put another sheet of baking paper on top and slightly flatten each yolk. Using a pasta machine, roll each cured yolk until it is 1 mm (1⁄16 in) thick. Using the fettuccine attachment, roll each sheet of yolk through the machine to create long noodles.

47-yolk tagliatelle
— *Serves 6*

The inspiration for this comes from superchef Massimo Bottura. I once cooked it for his book launch and named it quite pointedly, 'no fucking spaghetti in Bologna'. The world's most famous Italian dish, behind pizza, is spaghetti bolognese. People, do not order that in Italy. It will mark you as a pillock of the highest order. Spaghetti is from the south and Bologna is in the north and the twain never met. In the north they make ragu bolognese and they serve it with a fresh egg pasta called tagliatelle. Tagliatelle al ragu.

Ragu bolognese doesn't contain tomatoes, garlic or red wine. Some laws are immutable.

My favourite recipe for ragu comes from the classic 1954 book, Italian Food, *by Elizabeth David.*

---

1 kg (2 lb 3 oz/6⅔ cups) 00 flour

47 eggs (60 g/2 oz each)

butter to serve

freshly ground black pepper to serve

grated Parmigiano Reggiano to serve

Sift the flour into a pile on a work surface.

Carefully separate the yolks from the whites and reserve the whites for another use. Avoid any trace of yolk in the whites.

Make a well in the centre of the flour and add the yolks. Use the tips of your fingers to stir the yolks in a circular motion, incorporating the flour as you go to make a crumbly mass. Depending on the size of the eggs, humidity etc., you may need a tablespoon of water or so to achieve this.

Start to knead the mass with the heel of your hand. Knead for some minutes until the dough is smooth and silky and starts to relax.

Divide the dough into four and wrap it in plastic wrap. Refrigerate for 30 minutes to relax the dough.

Roll one of the dough quarters out by hand to around 5 mm (¼ in) thick.

Put the dough through the widest setting of your pasta machine. Fold the pasta in half and put it through again. Repeat this five or six times – the dough will start to look even-coloured and textured.

Lower the setting on the pasta machine and put the dough through again. Continue to the lowest setting. The dough will be getting quite long by now.

Dust the dough lightly with flour to stop it from sticking, and leave it to dry a little on the floured work surface. Repeat with the remaining dough.

Run the dough through the cutter to produce the tagliatelle, or roll up the sheet and cut it by hand with a sharp knife into 5 mm (¼ in) widths.

Cook the tagliatelle in lightly salted boiling water for 2–3 minutes, drain and serve with butter, pepper and Parmigiano Reggiano – or your favourite ragu.

You can make these tagliatelle in smaller quantities as suits your requirements.

CHAPTER FIFTEEN

Eggplant

Baba ghanoush

— Serves 4

A close relative of the tomato and potato, the eggplant (aubergine) is a staple ingredient in a diverse range of cultures. Since prehistoric times, it has been cultivated in South and East Asia, and the first known record of it is from a Chinese agricultural text dating from 544 AD. It was also grown in north Africa and was introduced to the Mediterranean area in the Middle Ages by Arab agriculturists.

Eggplant also happens to be my favourite fruit. It is the texture that is so satisfying. Coupled with its incredible versatility, I find it hard to beat.

---

1 large eggplant (aubergine)

100 ml (3½ fl oz) olive oil

2 garlic cloves, thinly sliced

2 thyme sprigs

½ teaspoon freshly ground cumin

Preheat the oven to 180°C (350°F).

Scorch the eggplant over a high gas flame or by using a kitchen blowtorch, to char the skin and create a smoky flavour.

Cut the eggplant in half lengthways and score the flesh in a criss-cross pattern. Brush each half liberally with olive oil.

Insert slices of garlic into the cuts, put a sprig of thyme on top and season well with salt and freshly ground black pepper.

Place the halves of the eggplant together and wrap in aluminium foil. Place on a baking tray and cook for 30 minutes.

Remove the eggplant from the oven and carefully unwrap it. Leave it until cool enough to handle.

Using a large spoon, scoop out the flesh and put it in a bowl with the cumin and remaining olive oil and whip to combine. This is best eaten on the day it's made, but will store for a couple of days.

Lee Ho Fook crispy eggplant
— Serves 4

This signature vegan dish from Marque alumni Victor Liong, is a combination of Chinese flavours from a traditional Taiwanese 'fish fragrant' eggplant sauce. However, it is made like a Korean fried chicken sauce to keep the batter of the eggplant crisp. This dish is a great representation of the cuisine at Victor's wonderful restaurant, Lee Ho Fook, and its multicultural birth is emblematic of what makes Australian cuisine great.

---

vegetable oil for deep-frying

2 large eggplants (aubergines)

10 coriander (cilantro) stems, chopped

1 long red chilli, seeded and sliced

2 spring onions (scallions), sliced

SPICED RED VINEGAR SAUCE

460 g (1 lb/2 cups) caster (superfine) sugar

100 g (3½ oz) liquid glucose

100 ml (3½ fl oz) soy sauce

70 g (2½ oz) soy paste

1 tablespoon Chinese black vinegar

2 teaspoons chilli bean paste

15 g (½ oz) fresh ginger, grated

3 garlic cloves, grated

½ teaspoon chilli powder

2 teaspoons Sichuan chilli paste

1 long red chilli, chopped

60 ml (2 fl oz/¼ cup) red rice vinegar

½ teaspoon ground Sichuan peppercorns

CRISPY BATTER

60 g (2 oz/⅓ cup) rice flour

60 g (2 oz) tapioca starch

10 g (¼ oz) xanthan gum

SESAME SALT

20 g (¾ oz) toasted sesame seeds

1 teaspoon sea salt

To make the spiced red vinegar sauce, put the sugar and glucose in a large saucepan over medium heat and bring to the boil slowly, whisking to combine and dissolve the sugar. Increase the heat to medium–high and cook until it forms a light caramel. Add the remaining sauce ingredients and 1 teaspoon salt and stir to combine. Bring back to the boil then reduce the heat to a simmer and cook for 15 minutes.

To make the crispy batter, blend 550 ml (18½ fl oz) water with the rice flour, tapioca starch, xanthan gum and 5 g (¼ oz) salt together in a high-speed blender to make a smooth, thick batter.

To make the sesame salt, blend the ingredients in a spice grinder to a coarse grain.

Preheat a deep-fryer or fill a large saucepan one-third full with vegetable oil and heat to 180°C (350°F).

Peel the eggplants and cut them into eighths lengthways.

Dip the eggplant strips in the batter and shake off any excess. Gently lower the strips into the hot oil, working with five to eight pieces at a time, and cook until golden and crispy, which will take around 5–10 minutes.

Transfer the eggplant to a bowl, add the sauce and stir gently to completely coat the eggplant pieces. Arrange the pieces on a serving plate and scatter over the chopped coriander stems, chilli and spring onion. Sprinkle over the sesame salt and serve immediately.

Steamed eggplant with sauce nero

— Serves 4

This is a relatively fancy recipe, albeit quite simple if you show a commitment to the cause. For some it may seem pointless, so turn the page and read on.

Cooking is about taking an ingredient that extra step, to unlock the potential of the produce and exaggerate its beauty. As the master chef Pierre Gagnaire said, 'Some chefs say they let the produce speak for itself. If you do little or nothing you end up with little or nothing.' A pithy observation.

STEAMED EGGPLANT

200 ml (7 fl oz) dark soy sauce

200 ml (7 fl oz) sherry vinegar

400 ml (13½ fl oz) extra-virgin olive oil

2 tablespoons cold-pressed sesame oil

1 garlic clove, finely chopped

1 large eggplant (aubergine)

SAUCE NERO

2 large eggplants (aubergines)

10 ml (¼ fl oz) sherry vinegar

To make the sauce nero, preheat the oven to 180°C (350°F).

Blacken the whole eggplants directly over a high gas flame or by using a kitchen blowtorch until well charred all over and the eggplants start to collapse.

Put the eggplants in a non-aluminium baking dish, cover the dish with foil and bake for 15 minutes.

Remove the eggplants from the oven and put them, together with any juices from the dish, in a fine sieve. Allow to drain for 2–3 hours. Reserve the liquid that has dripped through.

Remove the stems from the eggplants and purée the solids in a food processor until smooth.

Preheat the oven to 70°C (160°F) and line two baking trays with baking paper.

Spread the eggplant purée over the lined baking trays and place in the oven overnight until dry and crispy.

Once dry, blend the eggplant to a fine powder.

In a saucepan over medium heat, bring the reserved liquid to the boil with the sherry vinegar and a pinch of salt. Whisk in the eggplant powder then remove the pan from the heat.

Use a hand-held blender to process the sauce until thickened. Adjust the seasoning if required. Set aside.

To make the steamed eggplant, combine the soy sauce, vinegar, oils and garlic in a large bowl.

Remove the stem of the eggplant, then peel and cut the eggplant into eight even wedges. Place on a steamer tray, wrap tightly with plastic wrap and steam for 15–20 minutes or until the eggplant has the softness of marshmallow.

While still warm, add the eggplant to the marinade and leave overnight in the refrigerator to infuse.

To serve, warm the eggplant in the marinade. Drain and spoon the sauce nero over the top.

This recipe makes a delicious appetiser or an accompaniment to rich, fatty cuts of meat or fish.

CHAPTER SIXTEEN

—

Fish

Fish soup

— Serves 6

For me the south of France is a magical place. Or maybe it's the idea of it, as the romantic, sunny ideal of my mind's eye hasn't existed for a long time. It's a sunny paradise of days gone by, but I find it difficult to dismiss the rosy image. This recipe is a bit like that. I had a passing idea of the essence of this Mediterranean classic and the core elements and then made the rest up. I've cooked it for many years and feel no urge to change. Serve it with Rouille (page 46) and chargrilled sourdough bread.

---

1 kg (2 lb 3 oz) whole red mullet or scorpion fish

1 kg (2 lb 3 oz) snapper bones, or other white-fleshed fish bones, including the head

300 ml (10 fl oz) olive oil

1 teaspoon white peppercorns

2 star anise

100 ml (3½ fl oz) dry white wine

1 bay leaf

3 flat-leaf parsley sprigs

1 thyme sprig

1 carrot, peeled and cut into small dice

1 celery stalk, cut into small dice

1 onion, cut into small dice

1 fennel bulb, cut into small dice

1 small waxy potato, peeled and cut into small dice

6 ripe tomatoes

3 garlic cloves, crushed

100 ml (3½ fl oz) dry vermouth

50 ml (1¾ fl oz) Ricard or Pernod

1 pinch saffron threads

1 small red chilli

1 teaspoon sea salt

Scale the mullet and remove the guts. Reserve the liver and bones. Remove the lateral bones with a sharp knife and cut the mullet into rough pieces.

Wash the snapper bones and chop them coarsely.

Heat a heavy-based saucepan over medium heat and add 100 ml (3½ fl oz) of the olive oil. Add the snapper and mullet bones. Stir until the bones are caramelised and starting to fall apart. Add the peppercorns and star anise. Add the wine and reduce until it has fully evaporated. Cover with 1.5 litres (51 fl oz/6 cups) water and add the bay leaf, parsley and thyme. Bring to the boil then reduce the heat to a simmer and cook for 30 minutes to create a stock. Skim any grey scum that rises to the surface and discard.

Put another heavy-based saucepan over medium heat and add the remaining olive oil. Add the carrot, celery, onion, fennel and potato and sauté until lightly golden.

Core the tomatoes and process to a fine purée in a blender.

Add the crushed garlic to the vegetables and sauté for 30 seconds. Turn the heat to high and add the vermouth and Ricard. Reduce to a syrup, about 5 minutes, then add the tomato purée. Continue reducing until the olive oil starts to rise to the surface. Add the saffron, chilli, salt and a generous grinding of black pepper.

Place a very fine sieve over the pan and pour the fish stock through it. Discard the bones.

Bring to the boil and simmer briskly for 15 minutes. Add the reserved mullet (which will cook through in the heat of the soup). Do not skim any floating oil. Adjust the seasoning. Serve in a large bowl at the table and ladle into individual bowls.

Listen to 'Exile on Main Street' by the Stones, which was recorded at Villa Nellcôte, Villefranche-sur-Mer, Nice.

Brandade

— Serves 6–8

The regional cooking of France had me at bonjour. It is the beauty and elegance of cooking that was founded on pragmatism – the idea of prolonging the bounty of each particular season if there was surplus, and, if not, the profound act of staying alive.

This recipe is based on **brandade de morue** *(whipped salt cod) and the many iterations that exist in southern France.*

---

1 kg (2 lb 3 oz) white-fleshed fish fillet (such as cod, snapper, blue eye trevalla)

100 g (3½ oz) coarse sea salt

1 litre (34 fl oz/4 cups) milk

6 garlic cloves, crushed, plus an extra cut garlic clove to serve

4 fresh bay leaves

1 small bunch of thyme

300 g (10½ oz) waxy potatoes, such as desiree or dutch cream

200 ml (7 fl oz) extra-virgin olive oil, plus extra to serve

chargrilled sourdough bread to serve

Skin the fish and rub it all over using all the salt. Wrap it in plastic wrap and refrigerate for 12 hours.

Remove the fish from the refrigerator, unwrap it and rinse off the excess salt under cold running water.

Put the fish in a small saucepan over medium–low heat, cover with milk, add the crushed garlic, bay leaves and thyme and bring to a gentle simmer. Cook for 15 minutes until the fish starts to flake. Remove the fish, strain and reserve the milk and garlic.

Put the potatoes in a saucepan and cover with water. Bring to the boil over medium–high heat then reduce the heat to medium–low and simmer until tender. Drain the potatoes and peel them while they are still hot.

Flake the fish into a heavy-based saucepan and place over low heat.

Push the potatoes and garlic through a potato ricer, or sieve, straight into the pan with the fish. Beat the fish and potatoes together with a wooden spoon, while alternately adding the reserved milk and olive oil. Keep beating and adding the milk and olive oil until all the olive oil is used and a similar amount of milk. It should have the texture of mashed potato. Season with a good grinding of black pepper.

Serve a bowl of brandade with chargrilled sourdough bread rubbed with fresh garlic and olive oil.

Imported salt cod can be purchased, but I prefer to use local fish for a more delicate flavour and texture.

Kingfish ham

— Makes 2 sides, enough for 20

This fish, indigenous to the coastal waters of Australia, is properly known here as the yellowtail kingfish. But, in Australia, where nothing is called by its correct name, it's also known – depending where you are from – as albacore, bandit, hoodlum, king amberjack, kingfish, kingie, silver king, southern yellowtail, Tasmanian yellowtail, yellowtail, yellowtail amberjack and hiramasa.

I don't particularly think this fish cooks well, but it is superb as sashimi and for this type of application. This is beautiful with slices of ripe melon.

---

1 × 3–4 kg (6 lb 10 oz–8 lb 13 oz) kingfish

100 g (3½ oz) salt (per kg/2 lb 3 oz fish)

80 g (2¾ oz) sugar (per kg/2 lb 3 oz fish)

wood chips for smoking (hickory for preference)

Fillet and pin-bone the kingfish, leaving the skin on.

Mix the salt and sugar together in a bowl.

Take a tray the length of the fish and line it with plastic wrap, leaving enough overhang on all sides to wrap the fish. Place the two fish fillets on the tray side by side and cover each fillet with the salt and sugar cure.

Put the fillets on top of each other and wrap with the plastic wrap. Ensure that the fish is very tightly wrapped – another layer of plastic wrap may be required.

Leave the fish to cure in the refrigerator for 5–7 days, turning it each day so that it will cure evenly.

Once the fish has cured, carefully rinse it under cold running water and pat dry.

Cut down the centre line to produce four fillets – two shoulder, two belly.

Put the fillets, flesh side up, on a wire rack over a tray and put on the top rack of a cold oven. Leave the oven door open.

Fill an old ovenproof frying pan, which will fit in the oven, with wood chips. Place the pan of wood chips over high heat until they catch fire. Once alight, carefully shake the pan to disperse the chips and allow even burning. Once all the wood chips are burning, carefully put another ovenproof pan of the same size over the top of the first pan to snuff out the flames.

Put the pans inside the oven on the bottom shelf. Remove the top frying pan and quickly close the oven door, trapping the smoke inside. Leave for 5 minutes or until all the smoke has dissipated. Repeat this process three times using fresh wood chips each time.

After smoking, wrap the fish in muslin (cheesecloth) and refrigerate on a rack for 7–10 days. The belly hams will cure first due to their thickness. Use over the following month. They will also freeze well. Slice thinly before serving, if desired.

CHAPTER SEVENTEEN

—

Flour

Best ever banana bread

— Makes 1 loaf

Was there ever anything so pungently disappointing than a poor report and the forgotten locker banana at the end of school term?

The world is broken down into simple sub-sets – those who like ripe bananas and those who don't. I'm with the latter.

The dull grey shuffle of office life is surely not helped by the colon-blocking banality of commercial banana bread. This is something to do with bananas when the yellow starts to turn black. Cook and set yourself free.

---

250 g (9 oz) unsalted butter, cut into 1 cm (½ in) cubes and softened

335 g (12 oz) raw (demerara) sugar

4 eggs, at room temperature

1 cinnamon stick

1 star anise

2 cloves

3 cardamom pods

½ teaspoon white peppercorns

300 g (10½ oz/2 cups) plain (all-purpose) flour

3 teaspoons baking powder

6 ripe bananas

Freshly churned butter (page 103) to serve (optional)

Preheat the oven to 160°C (320°F). Grease a 21 × 6 × 1 cm (8¼ × 2½ × ½ in) loaf (bar) tin with butter and neatly line it with baking paper.

In the bowl of a stand mixer fitted with the paddle attachment, cream the butter and sugar on high speed. Add the eggs, one at a time, scraping down the side of the bowl after each addition.

In an electric spice grinder, or using a mortar and pestle, process the spices to a fine powder.

Sift the spices into a bowl with the flour and baking powder.

Peel and coarsely chop the bananas and toss them through the spiced flour mixture to coat.

Gently fold the flour and banana into the creamed butter and sugar until fully incorporated.

Pour the mixture into the prepared tin and tap once firmly on a work surface to remove any air pockets. Bake for 45–50 minutes or until a thermometer inserted in the centre reads 85°C (185°F). Allow to cool in the tin for 5 minutes before turning out onto a wire rack to cool completely.

Serve in slices with lashings of home-made or salted butter, if desired.

Coating the banana in the flour stops it from sinking to the bottom of the loaf.

Buttermilk high-top loaf

— Makes 2 loaves

The culinary timeline of white Australia is relatively short. In terms of bread, it is only very recently that the general population started to enjoy the delights of other cultures. I think it was 1990 before I had focaccia for the first time. Those were heady days, when everything was new.

As a country kid of the '70s, I would be sent to Nino's deli down the road for fresh bread. There were three choices: tank loaf, square loaf and high-top. Same bread, different shapes. This recipe trades on that memory and, with the addition of buttermilk, perhaps improves it.

1.2 litres (41 fl oz) buttermilk

1 kg (2 lb 3 oz/6⅔ cups) bread flour

500 g (1 lb 2 oz) plain (all-purpose/3⅓ cups) flour

15 g (½ oz) fresh yeast

15 g (½ oz) Murray River pink salt

Pour the buttermilk into the bowl of a stand mixer fitted with the dough hook.

Sift the flours together into a bowl. Rub the yeast into the flour then add the mixture to the buttermilk. Mix on slow speed until a rough dough forms. Add the salt and mix on medium speed for 15 minutes.

Place a clean cloth over the bowl and leave in a warm spot for 1½ hours or until the dough has doubled in size. If it's a cold day, warm the oven to 50°C (120°F), turn it off and put the bowl inside.

Turn the dough out onto a lightly floured work surface and divide it into two equal pieces. Roll each piece into a ball.

You will need two 23 × 13 × 7 cm (9 × 5 × 2¾ in) loaf (bar) tins.

Shape each ball into a loaf approximately the width of your tins. Place the loaves, seam side down, into the tins. Cover with a clean cloth and leave to prove in a warm place for another 1½ hours or until the dough reaches the tops of the tins.

Preheat the oven to 200°C (400°F).

Bake the loaves for 15 minutes until the top is dark golden. Reduce the heat to 170°C (340°F) and bake for a further 25 minutes or until the internal temperature reaches 90°C (194°F). Leave to cool in the tins for 10 minutes before turning out onto a wire rack to cool completely.

If you make our Freshly churned butter (page 103), you can make our bread, and the cycle continues.

Brioche

— Makes 20 brioche

'Let them eat cake.'

This mistranslation of a misattribution that folklore would have us believe started the French Revolution is commonly attributed to Marie Antoinette. She is purported to have said, **Qu'ils mangent de la brioche** *('let them eat brioche'). The peasantry had no money for bread, let alone this egg- and butter-enriched magnificence of the French boulangerie.*

---

750 g (1 lb 11 oz/5 cups) plain (all-purpose) flour

75 g (2¾ oz) caster (superfine) sugar

3 teaspoons salt

20 g (¾ oz) fresh yeast

9 eggs

450 g (1 lb) unsalted butter, cubed

EGG WASH

1 egg yolk

10 ml (¼ fl oz) milk

Put the flour, sugar and salt in the bowl of a stand mixer fitted with the dough hook. Crumble in the yeast and mix on medium speed until combined. Slowly add the eggs, one at a time, mixing well after each addition.

Once all the eggs are incorporated, begin to add the butter a few cubes at a time. Ensure each addition is fully incorporated before adding the next. Mix for a further 5 minutes until the mixture is smooth and glossy and has come away from the side of the bowl.

Remove the dough and place it in a greased stainless steel bowl. Cover with a damp tea towel (dish towel) and leave in the refrigerator for 24 hours to prove.

Remove the dough from the refrigerator and cut it into twenty 75 g (2¾ oz) portions.

Lightly grease 20 fluted 8 cm (3¼ in) moulds. Pinch off a little less than one-third of each portion of dough, for the tête (head). Roll the rest of the dough portions into a ball and press them into a prepared brioche mould. With lightly floured hands, shape each of the smaller dough pieces into an elongated pear shape. Using your index finger, make a hole in the centre of each brioche, going almost to the bottom of the mould, and insert the elongated part of the topknot deep into the hole. Cover the moulds loosely with oiled plastic wrap and let rise (ideally at 75–80°C/170–175°F) until the edges of the dough reach the tops of the moulds, about 1–1½ hours.

Preheat the oven to 220°C (430°F).

For the egg wash, lightly beat the yolk with the milk. Gently brush the tops of the brioche with the egg wash then bake for 10–15 minutes, until golden and the internal temperature reads 90°C (194°F) on a thermometer. The base should sound hollow when tapped. Turn out onto a wire rack to cool completely before serving.

This brioche dough can be formed into many shapes, each having a slightly different taste and texture due to the differing ratios of crust and crumb. A quick internet search of 'brioche mould' will show the variety.

Left to right: Brioche (page 141);
Buttermilk high-top loaf
(page 140)

CHAPTER EIGHTEEN

—

Honey

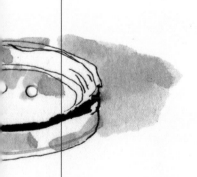

Honey biscuits

— Makes a lot

The smell of these biscuits baking brings a tear to my cynical eye. Nanna lived in Tanunda in the Barossa Valley and her family had lived there since the 1860s, after emigrating from Prussia and Silesia. She lived in a big old stone house built by her grandfather. Every year at Christmas time Nanna and Great Nanna would make these honey biscuits. We would always arrive green with travel sickness after rolling around the bench seat of the Holden. After a bit of fresh air and a 'glass of lemonade', the biscuit tin would come out and we could choose our 'shape' – little snowmen with white coats and sugared almonds, or ducks and rabbits with crunchy ears and silver cachou eyes.

---

900 g (2 lb) runny honey

450 g (1 lb) raw (demerara) sugar

4 whole eggs, plus 1 egg white

1.7 kg (3 lb 12 oz) plain (all-purpose) flour

1 teaspoon ground allspice

1 teaspoon ground cinnamon

½ teaspoon ground cloves

1 tablespoon bicarbonate of soda (baking soda)

sugared almonds to decorate

240 g (8½ oz) icing (confectioners') sugar

1 teaspoon lemon juice

In a small saucepan over low heat, warm the honey.

Transfer the honey to a very large bowl with the raw sugar and whole eggs. Gradually sift and stir in the flour, spices and bicarbonate of soda until you get a stiff mixture that is neither dry nor sticky. (The quantity of flour will vary slightly every batch.)

Cover the bowl with plastic wrap and leave overnight in the refrigerator.

Preheat the oven to 180°C (350°F) and line a baking tray with baking paper.

For simple round biscuits, roll 1 tablespoon of dough into a ball and place it on the lined baking tray. Flatten slightly.

Repeat with the remaining dough, leaving a 1 cm (½ in) space between the balls. Press a sugared almond into the top of each ball. (Alternatively, use decorative cookie cutters of your choice in various shapes.)

Bake for approximately 20 minutes or until the biscuits have a nice golden colour. Times will vary slightly depending on the thickness of the biscuit. A thin biscuit will be crisp while a ball will be softer.

Allow to set for a couple of minutes on the tray before transferring to a wire rack to cool.

While the biscuits are cooling, whisk the egg white in a bowl until just broken up. Whisk in the icing sugar to form a thin icing. Stir in the lemon juice to assist hardening the icing.

Decorate the cooled biscuits with the icing and leave for 25 minutes to set.

Tradition makes things taste better.

Honeycomb

— Makes one 20 × 20 cm (8 × 8 in) slab

Where too much is barely enough.

I once worked at Arpège for the mercurial M. Alain Passard. His mille-feuille was the reason I wanted to work there. Lighter than any puff pastry I'd ever had, it was like eating a block of crunchy bubbles. One of the secrets was to cut away most of the exterior to leave the caramelised honeycombed interior. It was this idea that I wanted to achieve with this confection. It took Lauren, pastry chef at Marque, and me some weeks to achieve the result. The recipe was everyday but it turns out, like everything else extraordinary, the secret was the sum of many tiny details. Serve with Crème fraiche (page 103) and 1 plus 1 = 3.

---

18 g (¾ oz) bicarbonate of soda (baking soda)

150 g (5½ oz) liquid glucose

65 g (2¼ oz) honey

415 g (14½ oz) caster (superfine) sugar

Line a 20 × 20 × 5 cm (8 × 8 × 2 in) baking tin with baking paper and warm it in a 100°C (210°F) oven.

Sift the bicarbonate of soda into a small bowl and set aside.

Put the glucose, honey, sugar and 75 ml (2½ fl oz) water in a large, deep, heavy-based saucepan and stir to combine. Wipe the side of the saucepan with a wet pastry brush to prevent any sugar from sticking to the side and burning. Turn the heat to medium – once the pan is on the heat, do not stir the sugar mixture as it will crystallise. Bring the mixture to 155°C (310°F). Immediately remove the pan from the heat and add the bicarbonate of soda all at once. Whisk quickly but thoroughly, ensuring the bicarbonate of soda is evenly dispersed through the sugar syrup. The mixture will instantly start to rise, but do not panic – whisk a little longer.

Pour the mixture into the prepared tin. The honeycomb will rise rapidly in the tin before setting. Do not move the tin before the honeycomb has had a chance to cool and set or the volume will disappoint.

Leave to cool for 1 hour minimum to achieve a hard-crack texture. Use a large serrated bread knife to remove the smooth outer layer and leave the aerated centre.

Honey madeleines

— Makes 10 large or 20 small madeleines

Madeleines seem to be inexorably glued to one of the most annoying and anodyne clichés in literature. As soon as madeleines are mentioned some arse will say, 'Ah, Proust!' – I think it makes them feel clever or maybe they are just being polite and inclusive. Anyway, whatever…while they are banging on about **Remembrance of Things Past** *(which they've never read) you may get on with the job of delivering these beauties hot from the oven.*

---

125 g (4½ oz) salted butter

zest of 1 lemon
(Meyer for preference)

3 eggs (60 g/2 oz)

130 g (4½ oz) caster (superfine)
sugar

30 g (1 oz) leatherwood honey

150 g (5½ oz/1 cup) plain
(all-purpose) flour

5 g (¼ oz) baking powder

Melt the butter with the lemon zest and leave to infuse for 10 minutes.

In the bowl of a stand mixer fitted with the whisk attachment, beat the eggs, sugar and honey until pale.

Sift the flour with the baking powder two or three times. Add it to the mixer and beat at high speed until very pale. Turn the mixer to low speed and add the melted butter in a slow steady stream.

Transfer the mixture to a piping (icing) bag and refrigerate for at least 12 hours (preferably 24) before use.

Preheat the oven to 190°C (375°F).

Lightly butter a non-stick madeleine tin and dust it with flour, tapping the mould on a work surface to remove any excess. Pipe each 'shell' two-thirds full. Place the tin in the oven and bake for 5–7 minutes until the centres rise like little volcanos and turn golden. These are best served immediately.

Larger 8 cm (3¼ in) madeleines cook best at 190°C (375°F) and petite 3 cm (1¼ in) madeleines are better at 210°C (410°F), but cooked for less time, which will give them a golden crust but not dry them out.

CHAPTER NINETEEN

—

Lamb

Roast lamb leg in chamomile

— *Serves 4 (plus leftovers for sandwiches)*

When designing dishes or looking for inspiration, it is most helpful to look at the natural environment of the main ingredient. More often than not it is nature that will suggest the best partner. Is it mere coincidence that the classic pairing of tomato and basil are also friends in the garden? In companion planting, basil is used as a natural pest-repellent to protect the ripening tomato. In the garden of the ocean, fish and seaweed are synonymous. If there is any better accompaniment for white-fleshed fish than seaweed butter I'm yet to find it.

So it is with lamb. I imagined the wee beast frolicking in the sun with zephyrs rushing through the spring grass and little white heads of chamomile nodding in agreement. Gee, they taste good together.

1.2 kg (2 lb 10 oz) suckling lamb leg (long leg, rump on)

2 teaspoons sea salt

1 garlic bulb, cloves separated and peeled

50 ml (1¾ fl oz) olive oil

50 g (1¾ oz) best-quality chamomile tea

2 onions, roots removed, cut into quarters

splash of white wine for deglazing

small bunch of fresh chamomile

Remove the lamb from the refrigerator 1 hour before preparation to allow more even cooking.

Preheat the oven to 180°C (350°F).

Evenly score the skin of the lamb to a depth of 5 mm (¼ in) and rub the salt all over the meat.

In a food processor, blend the garlic and olive oil into a paste, then rub this all over the lamb. Sprinkle over the chamomile tea leaves.

Heat a heavy roasting tin in the oven until hot.

Put the lamb and onion in the tin and cook for 1½ hours (25–30 minutes per 500 g/1 lb 2 oz), basting the meat with its fat from time to time. Cook the lamb to your preferred temperature (I prefer medium 65–70°C/149–158°F for the best flavour and texture). Remove the meat from the oven to rest for 20–30 minutes prior to serving.

Tip off some of the fat and deglaze the tin with a splash of white wine. Reduce the wine to nothing then add a little water. Bring to the boil, scraping the pan with a wooden spoon to make a jus and pour it over the sliced lamb to serve.

Garnish with the fresh chamomile flowers and carve the lamb at the table.

Lamb wrapped in fresh hay and baked is also splendid.

Lamb jerky

— Serves 4–6

In times past, if one killed a beast one had a couple of choices – eat as much as you could before it went off and/or the wolves got you. Or preserve it in some way to prolong its benefit and sanctify the slaughter of the poor beast.

Jerky is an American term and probably originated with the indigenous cultures of South America. The Boer of South Africa also preserved anything they could shoot as biltong, using sun and salt. These are a couple of examples I discovered in a pub as a young man.

---

4 fresh bay leaves, finely chopped

1 bunch of thyme, finely chopped

30 g (1 oz) coarse sea salt

10 g (¼ oz) raw (demerara) sugar

4 × 300 g (10½ oz) lamb rumps

1 teaspoon fennel seeds

1 teaspoon black peppercorns

1 teaspoon cumin seeds

1 star anise

Mix the bay leaves and thyme together with the salt and sugar.

Rub an equal amount of this dry marinade over each of the rumps. Wrap each rump in plastic wrap and refrigerate overnight.

Unwrap the parcels and pat the lamb dry. Place the meat in the freezer for around 2 hours to partially freeze it.

Remove the lamb from the freezer and slice each rump as thinly as possible, across the grain, using a very sharp knife or meat slicer if you have one. Place the sliced lamb on non-stick baking trays without any overlapping.

Preheat the oven to 50°C (120°F).

In a spice grinder, or using a mortar and pestle, grind the fennel seeds, peppercorns, cumin seeds and star anise to a fine powder. Using a tea strainer, sift the spice mixture over each piece of rump to evenly season it. Place the lamb in the oven and dry it overnight until crisp. Eat immediately or store for 2–3 days in an airtight container.

Use this technique for any type of meat (or fish). The herbs and spices are changeable as suits your desire.

Lamb hot pot
— Serves 4–6

This is just a delicious way to cook a lesser cut of meat. It renders a tougher cut unctuous and delicious. It is based on a Japanese home-style hot pot, hence the use of soy and daikon, both staples of that venerable culture. Lamb is not that common in Japan but is a relatively recent and well-loved ingredient on the northern island of Hokkaido. This recipe works equally well with pork shoulder and belly, which probably belies the recipe's Chinese origin.

1 kg (2 lb 3 oz) boneless lamb shoulder

400 g (14 oz) daikon (white radish)

200 ml (7 fl oz) naturally fermented dark Japanese soy sauce

100 ml (3½ fl oz) mirin

50 g (1¾ oz) raw (demerara) sugar

2 cm (¾ in) piece fresh ginger, sliced

1 teaspoon black peppercorns

Cut the lamb shoulder into six to eight large pieces.

Peel the daikon and also cut it into six to eight pieces.

Put the lamb in a saucepan over high heat with enough water to cover and bring to the boil. Remove the lamb from the pan and discard the water.

Transfer the lamb to a heavy, flameproof casserole and add the daikon and remaining ingredients. Add 1 litre (34 fl oz/4 cups) water to cover – or more if required. Bring quickly to a low simmer over medium heat and skim any impurities that rise to the surface. Reduce to a very low simmer and put on a tight-fitting lid. Cook for 2–2½ hours until the lamb is just falling apart. Serve from the casserole dish.

CHAPTER TWENTY

—

Mushrooms

Fermented shiitake mushrooms

— Serves 4

Mushrooms have an ability to satisfy in the same way that meat can and, like meat, they are completely transformed when cooked and bring an intensity that other vegetables lack. Fermentation is something of a revelation in terms of its effect on taste and texture with fruits and vegetables. I love shiitake for their intense savoury smell when raw and also their robust texture. The magic of fermentation turns them into an intensely savoury umami bomb.

---

12 shiitake mushrooms

1 litre (34 fl oz/4 cups) filtered water

1 slice sourdough bread

Put the mushrooms in a container and add the filtered water to just cover them.

Weigh the mushrooms and water and add 2% of the total weight in salt (less the weight of the container).

Add the bread to the mushrooms and water and cover with baking paper.

Use a plate to weigh the mushrooms down to ensure they remain submerged in the water while fermenting.

Leave at room temperature for 5–7 days. The time will vary depending on the size of the mushrooms. Larger mushrooms will take longer to ferment.

Once the mushrooms have taken on a pleasant sour taste, remove the plate, baking paper and sourdough bread and discard the paper and bread.

To serve, bring the mushrooms to room temperature in the fermenting liquid. If the mushrooms are exposed to air for too long they will oxidise.

Store in the refrigerator in the fermenting liquid. They will keep for 3–4 weeks.

Serve as an able partner to meat and fish or thinly sliced with grilled mushrooms.

Stuffed mushrooms

— Serves 4

One of my enduring memories is mushroom-picking with my poppa. It was in a quintessentially Australian landscape and in that way couldn't be more different from the European experience. The green rolling hills around the Barossa Valley are cleared for grazing and dotted with huge old gum trees. With the right combination of sun and rain, these field mushrooms would push through the grass and would be the size of my hand. The pristine white caps would stand in stark relief from the green grass and we would cut the caps from the ground with a small knife to ensure next year's crop. Poppa would chop them into a big pot and cook them with milk, salt and pepper. He'd thicken the sauce with cornflour (cornstarch) and serve them on slabs of buttered white toast. 'Mushies on toast', I can still taste them.

---

8 extra-large field (portobello) mushrooms

1 garlic clove, finely chopped

1 onion, finely chopped

100 g (3½ oz) butter

50 ml (1¾ fl oz) vermouth

1 bunch of curly parsley

8 sage leaves

1 teaspoon sea salt flakes

1 teaspoon freshly ground white pepper

4 duck livers

Choose the four best mushrooms and carefully remove their stalks.

Place the remaining mushrooms and reserved stalks in a food processor and pulse to a coarse mince or pâté.

In a frying pan over medium heat, sauté the garlic and onion in a little of the butter until golden. Add the remaining butter and minced mushrooms and cook over high heat, stirring, until most of the liquid has evaporated. Add the vermouth and cook for another minute.

Wash the parsley very well and pick the leaves from the stalks. Chop the parsley leaves with the sage. Add the herbs to the mushroom mixture in the pan and season with the salt and pepper.

Season the duck livers and, in a separate frying pan, sauté them over high heat to caramelise each side.

Preheat the oven to 180°C (350°F).

Place the reserved mushrooms, cup side up, on a baking tray and place a duck liver into each. Distribute the mushroom pâté over the livers and fill the mushroom cups evenly. Bake for 15 minutes, or until golden. Serve as they are, or as a side to roast duck.

Mushroom consommé

— Serves 4

Consommé is one of the classical measures of a chef's talent. There is nowhere to hide. The clarity and flavour must be precise. It is the essence of your ingredient. Traditionally, consommés were meat based, the clarification coming from a raft of minced (ground) meat, vegetables and sometimes egg white. This method tends to bring a certain base sameness to the table. Nowadays I tend not to put any vegetable other than the odd onion in my stocks to give them distinction from each other. This recipe is a more contemporary approach to a clear broth with nothing to mitigate the pure mushroom flavour.

---

1 kg (2 lb 3 oz) button mushrooms

2 French shallots

1 garlic clove

2 cm (¾ in) piece fresh ginger

1 teaspoon white peppercorns

1 clove

100 ml (3½ fl oz) white soy sauce

2 teaspoons arrowroot starch

Place all the ingredients, except the soy sauce and arrowroot, in a food processor and pulse to a fine mince.

Transfer the mixture to a large, heavy-based saucepan with 1 litre (34 fl oz/4 cups) water and the soy sauce. Cook over low heat for 2 hours.

Decant the liquid through a coffee filter, pressing down lightly on the solids. Discard the solids.

Whisk the arrowroot with 1 tablespoon water. Whisk this mixture into the broth, return everything to the pan and bring to a low simmer – it should thicken slightly.

If you have nimble fingers, make tiny little ravioli using the mushroom solids as the stuffing. Serve with the consommé poured over.

—

CHAPTER TWENTY-ONE

Parsnips

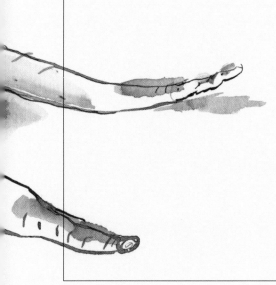

Sweet and savoury parsnip chips

— Serves 4

On a slow news day in 2009, a famous Australian TV gardening guru and an equally famous cookery author went to war – over the humble parsnip. The guru described the author as 'wretched' for serving parsnips to people, as they were not fit for pigs. 'I'm outraged, I'm angry, I'm upset, I'm crushed. I'm all of those things and a lot more,' he said on air. He insisted that they (the poor parsnips) 'were an affront to human dignity. I respect pigs, I like pigs, but I wouldn't give my pet pig parsnips.'

The author and the parsnip industry rose up to defend the worthy vegetable. The author said the guru was 'out of touch' and sent him a box of parsnips with recipes, challenging him to confront his prejudices.

'I was surprised he was having a go. It's just a parsnip,' the author said. 'If the guru cared to step into a modern restaurant he would find everyone's using parsnips – they're in vogue.'

Not only 'in vogue', Madam. Bloody delicious.

SWEET PARSNIP CHIPS

2 large parsnips, peeled

500 g (1 lb 2 oz) sugar

SAVOURY PARSNIP CHIPS

2 large parsnips

vegetable oil for frying

Murray River pink salt

For the sweet parsnip chips preheat the oven to 50°C (120°F) and line a baking tray with baking paper.

Carefully slice the parsnips as thinly as possible using a mandoline.

In a saucepan over medium–high heat, bring the sugar and 1 litre (34 fl oz/4 cups) water to the boil. Reduce the heat to a low simmer and add the sliced parsnips. Cook for 15 minutes or until soft, but not falling apart.

Strain the parsnips through a colander and drain.

Place the parsnip chips on the lined baking tray and bake for 2–3 hours or until dry and crisp.

For the savoury parsnip chips, carefully slice the parsnips as thinly as possible using a mandoline.

Heat the vegetable oil to 160°C (320°F) in a deep-fryer or deep saucepan and fry the parsnips until lightly golden. Drain on paper towel and sprinkle with pink salt to serve.

Savoury parsnip chips (top);
Sweet parsnip chips (bottom)

Parsnip cornetto

— Makes 10

So we were playing around with lime-soaking and vegetables. We baked the parsnip and ended with quite a soft vegetable with a leathery skin – not very tasty and not very attractive. Seemingly wasted endeavour. Not one to give up on anything, I cut off the end and squeezed out the middle. My feeble mind started to clear. It looked a little like an ice cream cone and from there it was short work to make it crisp, and with a little icing sugar and a lick of flame we had our eureka moment.

PARSNIP CONES

100 g (3½ oz) hydrated lime powder (common builder's lime)

5 litres (170 fl oz/20 cups) filtered water

10 parsnips, 4–5 cm (1½–2 in) diameter at thickest part, peeled

1 litre (34 fl oz/4 cups) vegetable oil for frying

icing (confectioners') sugar to dust

PARSNIP ICE CREAM

500 g (1 lb 2 oz) parsnip trimmings and pulp left over from the cones

150 g (½ oz) butter, cut into small pieces

1 litre (34 fl oz/4 cups) milk

100 g (3½ oz) caster (superfine) sugar

10 egg yolks

To make the parsnip cones, using a wooden spoon, combine the lime powder and filtered water in a plastic container. Carefully place the peeled parsnips in the water, ensuring they are completely covered. Leave to soak for 3 hours. Agitate the water every 10–15 minutes as the lime powder will settle on the bottom of the container.

Preheat the oven to 140°C (275°F). Remove the parsnips from the lime water and rinse them thoroughly with cold water. Pat dry with paper towel. Bake on a wire rack on a baking tray for 2 hours – turn the parsnips every 10–15 minutes to ensure they dry evenly on all sides.

Once baked, cut off the top of the parsnips and scoop out all of the parsnip flesh with a small utility knife. The lime will have created a thin leathery crust. Reserve the flesh for making the ice cream.

To make the parsnip ice cream, preheat the oven to 180°C (350°F). Put the parsnip trimmings and pulp and butter in a roasting tin and roast for 20–30 minutes until dark golden. Remove from the oven and, while still warm, pour over the milk. Cover with plastic wrap and leave in the refrigerator overnight to infuse.

Pass the parsnip mix through a fine sieve. Check the volume of milk and, if necessary, add a little more to bring the total to 1 litre (34 fl oz/4 cups).

Put the parsnip milk and half the sugar in a saucepan over high heat and stir to partially dissolve the sugar. The undissolved sugar will sink to the bottom of the saucepan and prevent the milk from burning. While the milk and sugar mixture is coming to the boil, whisk the egg yolks and the remaining sugar in a large bowl until well combined. Once the milk and sugar mixture has come to the boil, slowly pour half the liquid into the yolks while whisking.

Return the yolk and milk mixture back to the saucepan, whisking constantly. Reduce the heat to medium–low. Whisk continually until the mixture reaches 80°C (176°F).

Strain the milk through a fine sieve into a metal bowl and place over an ice bath. Whisk the ice cream base as it is cooling to allow the heat to escape and distribute the cooler liquid from the outside of the bowl into the mixture. Once fully cooled, churn in an ice cream machine following the manufacturer's instructions.

To serve, fill a small saucepan or deep-fryer with the oil and fry the parsnip 'skin' for the cones at 170°C (340°F) until lightly golden.

Dust with icing sugar and caramelise with a blowtorch to form a golden crust. To finish, top each cone with a scoop of parsnip ice cream and serve immediately.

See page 13 for more information on hydrated lime powder.

Parsnip cake

— Serves 4

Parsnips are not normally associated with cake. Having said that, I'd imagine that carrots weren't always either. For me the carrot cake has now reached a level of banality where I would rather saw off an appendage than submit to a piece. It was from this dark emotional place that the parsnip cake had its inception. This cake, if carefully made, is a revelation in terms of the sweet, moist nuttiness and perhaps, counter-intuitively, the delicacy the parsnip brings to the game.

175 g (6 oz) unsalted butter

250 g (9 oz) raw (demerara) sugar

100 g (3½ oz) golden syrup (light treacle)

3 eggs

250 g (9 oz/1⅔ cups) plain (all-purpose) flour

1 tablespoon baking powder

350 g (12½ oz) parsnips

ICING

1 egg white

240 g (8½ oz) icing (confectioners') sugar

1 teaspoon lemon juice

Preheat the oven to 160°C (320°F). Grease a non-stick 22 × 10 cm (8¾ × 4 in) ring (bundt) tin.

In a large saucepan over low heat, melt the butter, sugar and golden syrup. Remove from the heat and allow the mixture to cool for 5 minutes.

Lightly whisk the eggs and add them to the cooled mixture.

Sift together the flour and baking powder.

Peel and coarsely grate the parsnips. Toss in the flour mixture to coat.

Combine the wet ingredients with the dry ingredients and pour into the prepared tin. Bake for 40–45 minutes or until an inserted skewer comes out clean.

Turn out onto a wire rack and leave to cool for 15–20 minutes before icing.

To make the icing, whisk the egg white in a medium bowl until just broken up. Whisk in the icing sugar to form a thin icing. Stir in the lemon juice to assist hardening.

Decorate the cooled cake with the icing and leave for 25 minutes to set before serving.

Serve with a delicate loose-leaf black tea.

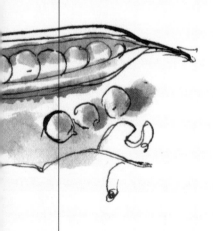

CHAPTER TWENTY-TWO

—

Peas

Pea and ham soup

— Serves 8

I can't remember a time when this wasn't on the winter home dinner roster. It's a family staple. It's one of those perfect and complete soups that nourishes, warms and invigorates. I've used smoked ham hock for its delicious balance of salt, smoke and gelatinous flesh. Mum used to use bacon bones and, as a very seasonal treat, the bone from the Christmas ham. (I tell you, that ham was the gift that just kept giving and giving and…) Bacon bones are good but a little salty so you must blanch them first and discard the water. The best version I ever made was from the offcuts of a jamón ibérico and fresh peas. So good.

---

500 g (1 lb 2 oz) packet green split peas

1 × 500 g (1 lb 2 oz) smoked ham hock

2 onions, finely chopped

2 large carrots, peeled and finely chopped

1 bunch of mint

1 bunch of marjoram

2 teaspoons freshly ground white pepper

Rinse the split peas and add them to a 4 litre (135 fl oz/16 cup) stockpot with the ham hock. Cover with water and bring to the boil. Turn down to a simmer and skim any froth from the surface.

Add the onion and carrot to the pot.

Tie the herbs together in a tidy bunch using butcher's string then add them to the pot along with the white pepper. Put a lid on and simmer slowly for 5–6 hours until the peas have broken down completely and the hock meat has come away from the bone. Remove and discard the herbs.

Remove the ham hock and debone it. Discard the bones. Chop the meat and skin into bite-sized pieces. Return it all to the stockpot and serve immediately. Any leftovers are suitable for freezing.

Make double the amount as it freezes exceptionally well.

Socca

— Serves 4

I first came across this recipe via the writings of a Niçois native, M. Alain Ducasse, where he served it with some irony to the well-heeled customers of his restaurant, Louis XV. Nice has flip-flopped over history under the flags of France and Italy, so it is no surprise to find this type of preparation is found all the way down the coast to Sicily, where it is known as panella. In Tuscany, it is known as cecina (torta di ceci or farinata), and it is a pizza-shaped snack served with different toppings like pizza. It's also a traditional food from Pisa and Livorno, which you can also find in many other cities of the Tyrrhenian coast. In La Spezia it's called farinata and in Savona, fainà. All are made the same way with perhaps slightly different ratios of besan (chickpea flour), olive oil and water. Mine has the addition of yeast to give it a fluffier texture. Not traditional but that is how cuisine rolls, ever changing, morphing and adapting.

---

5 g (¼ oz) fresh yeast

100 ml (3½ fl oz) warm water

90 g (3 oz) besan (chickpea flour)

2 g (¹⁄₁₀ oz) salt

3 teaspoons olive oil

butter for brushing

virgin olive oil for drizzling

sea salt flakes to garnish

thyme sprigs to garnish

Preheat the oven to 180°C (350°F).

In a bowl, mix together the fresh yeast, warm water, besan and 1 teaspoon of the olive oil with a hand-held blender. Once the yeast is incorporated into the mixture, blend in the salt. Cover the bowl and place it in a warm spot for 1 hour.

Heat the remaining olive oil in a small cast-iron frying pan over medium–high heat. Once the pan is hot, use a small ladle to pour in the socca mixture. Cook for 1–2 minutes until the bottom is caramelised. Flip the socca over and brush the top with butter.

Transfer to a baking tray and place in the oven for 5 minutes to cook through. Serve immediately, sprinkled with a little virgin olive oil and some sea salt flakes and garnished with thyme sprigs.

Fermented hummus and falafel

— Serves 4

If you buy hummus from the supermarket in one of those little plastic containers, take a minute to look at the ingredients. They may look similar to those below save one; preservatives. Due to the magic of fermentation, when the acidity rises due to naturally occurring lactic acid-fermenting organisms, many other pathogenic micro-organisms are killed. Not only that, it tastes good.

FERMENTED HUMMUS

1 kg (2 lb 3 oz) dried chickpeas

3 g (¹⁄₁₀ oz) ground cumin

30 g (1 oz) sea salt

150 ml (5 fl oz) olive oil, plus extra for finishing

180 ml (6 fl oz) lemon juice

125 g (4½ oz) tahini

FALAFEL

200 g (7 oz) dried chickpeas

1 teaspoon coriander seeds

1 teaspoon cumin seeds

15 g (½ oz) curly parsley

15 ml (½ fl oz) lemon juice

zest of 1 lemon

250 g (9 oz/1 cup) fermented hummus (see above)

30 g (1 oz) besan (chickpea flour)

vegetable oil for frying

For the fermented hummus put the chickpeas in a large bowl and cover them with water. Leave to soak in the refrigerator overnight. Put the chickpeas and soaking liquid to cover in a pressure cooker. Cook for 1 hour on high pressure until soft (or simmer for 2½ hours in a conventional pot).

Once soft, blend the chickpeas with 200 ml (7 fl oz) of the cooking liquid, the cumin, sea salt, olive oil, lemon juice and tahini until a thick purée forms.

Transfer the mixture to a sterilised airtight glass jar and pour a 2 cm (¾ in) layer of olive oil on top. Leave the hummus to ferment at room temperature until it starts to break through the surface oil – this will take about a week. It should then be refrigerated and can be eaten as is or used in the falafel below.

For the falafel put the chickpeas in a large bowl and cover them with water. Leave to soak in the refrigerator overnight. Put the chickpeas and soaking liquid to cover in a pressure cooker. Cook for 1 hour on high pressure until soft (or simmer for 2½ hours in a conventional pot).

Use a food processor to process all the ingredients, except the fermented hummus, besan and oil, to a coarse purée. Mix in the fermented hummus and besan by hand.

Roll the mixture into bite-sized balls.

Fill a saucepan one-third full of vegetable oil and heat to 180°C (350°F). Fry the balls until golden then transfer to paper towel to drain. Serve hot with the hummus.

—

CHAPTER TWENTY-THREE

Pork

Brawn

— Serves 10

One man's lunch is another man's, 'Oh my god, that's disgusting!' Again it is a reflex stemming from the disassociation with the food's provenance. Brawn is delicious and something I've eaten since I was a child, and actually started making from my first days in a commercial kitchen. I've always enjoyed its gelatinous savouriness and the pungent cut of curly parsley. As a side note, I would just like to say curly parsley rocks and should never be substituted by the flat-leaf variety. They are different things. Anyway; if you don't like things with heads or eyes, it might just be time to get over it.

---

1 pig's head, brain removed,
cut in half

1 smoked ham hock

1 large onion, coarsely chopped

1 large carrot, peeled and
coarsely chopped

1 celery stalk

2 teaspoons white peppercorns

1 bottle dry Riesling

1 large bunch of curly parsley

100 g (3½ oz) capers,
coarsely chopped

200 g (7 oz) cornichons,
coarsely chopped

50 g (1¾ oz) sea salt

Soak the pig's head in cold water overnight with two handfuls of salt.

Drain and place the pig's head in a 5 litre (170 fl oz/20 cup) stockpot with the ham hock. Cover with cold water and bring to the boil.

Drain, rinse the head and hock and return the meat to the cleaned pot. Add the onion, carrot, celery and peppercorns. Add the Riesling and then top up with enough water to cover the meat. Bring to the boil, skimming any impurities that rise to the surface. Simmer gently for 3–3½ hours until the pig's head is tender.

Carefully remove the head and hock and leave them to cool.

Pass the cooking liquor through a fine sieve into a clean pan over medium heat. Cook until the liquid is reduced by two-thirds, skimming any impurities that rise to the surface.

Test the set of the liquor by refrigerating a little in a saucer until set – you are looking for a firm jelly. Reduce the liquor more as required. (See note.)

Pick the meat and skin from the bones, including the tongue and fat from the head, and chop very coarsely. Discard the bones.

Pick the parsley leaves and discard the stalks. Wash the parsley in several changes of cold water, drain well, then chop coarsely.

In a large bowl, mix the meat, parsley, capers, cornichons and half the reduced liquor until well combined. Check for seasoning and add salt as required – it should be well seasoned.

Use a large slotted spoon to fill a 2 litre (68 fl oz/8 cup) terrine with the mixture, making sure the ingredients are evenly distributed. Add the remaining liquor to cover by 1 cm (½ in). Refrigerate overnight to set.

Depending on the shape of the terrine, you can serve the brawn straight from this with a large spoon or, if you have a rectangular mould you can warm the sides and tip the brawn onto a serving platter to be served sliced. (Just be aware that if you do this, the brawn needs a very firm set, so you can add leaf gelatine to firm it up.)

Pork and fennel sausages

— Makes 20–30

I started making my own sausages some 20 years ago as the local butchers then, with a few exceptions, were a little slow to get on board with the changing culinary environment. In my childhood I grew to love artisanal, German-style 'smallgoods', and as a young chef it was a natural thing to make my own sausages when the quality wasn't available. There is a lot of beautiful artisanal products available now, but we still make our own otherwise it's just shopping, and where's the fun in that?

3.5 kg (7 lb 12 oz) pork shoulder

1.1 kg (2 lb 7 oz) pork back fat

2 garlic bulbs

50 g (1¾ oz) fennel seeds

50 g (1¾ oz) black peppercorns

50 g (1¾ oz) table salt

3.5 g (⅛ oz) saltpetre

15 g (½ oz) fresh rosemary

335 ml (11½ fl oz) white wine

3 m (9 ft 10 in) natural thick pork sausage casing

Remove the skin and trim any excess fat and sinew from the pork shoulder. Cut the meat into strips and chill in the refrigerator for 1 hour.

Cut the pork back fat into 1 cm (½ in) cubes and also chill in the refrigerator for 1 hour.

Preheat the oven to 180°C (350°F).

Put the garlic bulbs on a baking tray and roast them for 20 minutes or until soft. Peel and set aside.

Heat a dry frying pan over medium heat. Add the fennel seeds and cook until fragrant. Keep half of the seeds whole and set them aside. Transfer the other half of the seeds to a spice grinder and finely blend them with the black peppercorns, table salt, saltpetre and rosemary. Add the roasted garlic to the spice mixture and stir to combine.

Coarsely mince (grind) the pork shoulder and back fat together – ensure the pork remains cold.

Combine the spice mixture, whole fennel seeds, white wine and pork by hand, keeping the mixture as cold as possible. (It may be necessary to refrigerate the mixture during the process to maintain the temperature.) Let the mixture marinate for a day in the refrigerator.

Tie one end of the sausage casing and feed the casing onto the sausage funnel of your mincer (grinder). Fill the casing, tying in 15 cm (6 in) lengths, and hang in the refrigerator for 2 days to firm and dry.

Saltpetre: This cure blend consists of salt, sodium nitrite and in some cases a pink or red colour to differentiate it from standard salt. The nitrite keeps the meat safe for a short period of time, and retains the natural red meat colour. This is used in products that are made and then cooked and eaten quickly like fresh sausages. It is readily available online.

Boudin noir

— Serves 6–8

It is unfortunate that as consumers we are losing or have lost the connection between our food and its source. Even in the butchery trade and professional kitchen, it is becoming unusual to see meat in a recognisable form as in an entire carcass. There is something to be said for rearing and slaughtering your own food for the respect and understanding that is generated by this intimate involvement. Blood is a source of protein and deliciousness that really can't be beaten and is revered and enjoyed by many cultures, although perhaps not so much in our insular, affluent society. These days there are so many options for those who can afford to have principles.

---

75 g (2¾ oz) pork back fat, diced

500 g (1 lb 2 oz) onions, diced

500 g (1 lb 2 oz) pig's blood

125 ml (4 fl oz/½ cup) pouring (single/light) cream

15 g (½ oz) salt

15 g (½ oz) quatre-épices

10 g (¼ oz) hot paprika

3 g (¹⁄₁₀ oz) chilli powder

75 g (2¾ oz) fresh sourdough breadcrumbs

2 m (6½ ft) thick natural pork casing

Begin the recipe a day ahead.

In a frying pan over medium heat, cook the pork back fat until it has rendered by half. Add the onion and sweat until soft, avoiding any caramelisation.

In a large bowl, combine the pork back fat, onion and the remaining ingredients, except the casings. Cover and refrigerate overnight.

Tie one end of the sausage casing and feed the casing onto the sausage funnel of your mincer (grinder) then fill the casing. Tie the end making sure that the casing is not too tight as the filling expands when cooked. This is hard to explain so there may be the odd failure (that's cooking).

Poach in a large saucepan of water at 85°C (185°F) for 50 minutes or until set. Remove the pan from the heat and leave to cool for an hour before transferring the sausage to a tray. Refrigerate.

To serve, cut off lengths as required and then gently pan-fry or grill.

The name quatre-épices literally means 'four spices'. The spice mix contains equal quantities of ground white pepper, cloves, nutmeg and ginger. This ratio is often adjusted to suit taste and requirement.

Left to right: Pork and fennel sausages (page 188); Boudin noir (page 189)

CHAPTER TWENTY-FOUR

—

Potatoes

Potato mash

— *Serves 4*

Joël Robuchon was once voted 'chef of the century'. He would often quip that his reputation was made on his green salad and mashed potato. It was while working for one of his alumni that I learnt the fine art of pomme purée. *The secret is in the quality of the potato, the quality and amount of butter (M. Robuchon's recipe is almost 50 per cent butter!), good old-fashioned elbow grease and a light seasoning from the sweat of your brow. This recipe is a little more user friendly (in terms of the heart-stopping quantities of butter) and being 'allowed' to use a whisk. I lost many layers of skin from the palm of my hand using the required wooden spoon.*

---

500 g (1 lb 2 oz) dutch cream potatoes, or any high-quality waxy potato

rock salt

165 ml (5½ fl oz) milk

165 g (6 oz) cold unsalted butter, diced

Murray River pink salt

Preheat the oven to 230°C (445°F).

Wash the potatoes under cold running water and pat them dry.

Fill the base of a roasting tin with rock salt. Put the potatoes in the tin and cover with aluminium foil. Bake for 45 minutes or until fully cooked through.

While still hot, remove the potato skins with the back of a small knife.

Pass the warm potatoes through a potato ricer.

Warm the milk in a small saucepan over medium heat.

Put the potato in a large saucepan over medium heat with half the warm milk. Gradually whisk in the cold butter. Adjust the thickness of the mash with the remaining milk. Whisk quite vigorously to develop a nice shine on the potato. Season with pink salt to taste.

Pass the mash through a drum sieve. Serve hot. If necessary, reheat the mash with a little milk before serving.

Potato chips

— Serves 4

As a professional chef I'm often asked what I like to eat; what is my 'go to' dish in my down time? I usually reply with a dish of elegance and intrigue, as befitting my high status in the industry. However, my dirty secret, good people, is chips (crisps). I just love them. Salt and vinegar for preference and a big bag and I don't share. So there it is. Judge me if you will. These chips made from good potatoes in season are delicious and robust in flavour and texture. They make an excellent accompaniment to dips, steak tartare or with a cold pint of your poison.

---

3 large sebago potatoes

1 litre (34 fl oz/4 cups) vegetable oil for frying

1 teaspoon sea salt or to taste

Preheat the oven to 90°C (195°F).

Put the potatoes in a baking dish lined with baking paper and bake for 1 hour. Remove from the oven and cool. (This sets the starch of the potato making them easier to slice and allowing them to brown more evenly.)

Using a mandoline, carefully slice the potato to a thickness of 3 mm (⅒ in).

Heat the vegetable oil in a shallow saucepan or deep-fryer to 160°C (320°F).

Fry the potato slices until golden brown then transfer to paper towel to drain. Season with sea salt to taste.

Stir-fried potatoes

— Serves 4

Quite a few years ago I enjoyed or, to be more accurate, survived a walk along the Great Wall of China. A combination of soft lifestyle, altitude and the grey haze of industrial China had me puffing like a one-legged man in an arse-kicking contest. There was further ignominy and no relief to be had when an ancient crone tried to sell me a beer from the cart she had hauled out there herself.

Salvation was at hand with a delightful lunch on the return home. The dishes were simple and surprising and based on the most remarkably modest ingredients – carrot, cabbage, potato.

The potato dish was in itself a revelation in that it was slightly crunchy and delicate – attributes not usually associated with the common spud in Western cuisine. For the recipe I refer to **Every Grain of Rice** *by the acknowledged expert on the subject, the delightful and erudite Fuchsia Dunlop.*

---

4 large waxy potatoes

60 ml (2 fl oz/¼ cup) sesame oil

4 dried chillies

1 teaspoon Sichuan peppercorns

½ teaspoon salt

½ teaspoon sugar

Peel the potatoes and cut them into very thin slices. Lay the slices flat and cut them into very fine matchstick slivers. Soak them for a few minutes in plenty of cold, lightly salted water to remove the excess starch.

Season a wok, then add 2 tablespoons of the sesame oil and swirl it around over medium–high heat until hot but not smoking.

Add the dried chillies and Sichuan peppercorns and stir-fry briefly until the oil is fragrant and spicy. Add the potato, turn the heat up to high and stir-fry vigorously for 4–5 minutes. When the potatoes are hot and cooked but still al dente and not coloured, remove them from the heat. Stir in the remaining sesame oil and serve.

The finer and more evenly you cut the potatoes the better the result. Use a Japanese mandoline if you wish, although this will not hone your knife skills.

CHAPTER TWENTY-FIVE

—

Pumpkin

Pumpkin soup
— *Serves 6*

I hesitate to do this to my mum as I upset her by a mildly disparaging mention in my last book. Anyway … I watched her make pumpkin soup which, bravo kiss kiss, she did quickly and efficiently using just pumpkin and water and some seasoning. The issue was the flavour – i.e., none.

A good dish is the accumulation of many details and gathering layers of flavour to create depth and integrity. The pumpkin actually requires a reasonable amount of assistance to give it substance. I was once asked, 'What makes your pumpkin soup better?' Two things, taste and texture.

---

1 small ripe Queensland blue pumpkin (winter squash), or any firm, orange-fleshed variety

1 onion, coarsely chopped

2 garlic cloves, coarsely chopped

200 g (7 oz) salted butter

1 teaspoon salt

½ teaspoon freshly ground white pepper

¼ teaspoon freshly grated nutmeg

100 ml (3½ fl oz) white wine

1 litre (34 fl oz/4 cups) chicken stock

Cut the pumpkin into large wedges and remove the seeds and skin. Cut it into even-sized cubes.

In a saucepan over low heat, cook the onion and garlic in the butter until translucent. Add the salt, pepper and nutmeg. Increase the heat to medium and add the pumpkin. Cook until the butter splits and the pumpkin starts to colour. Add the wine and cook until reduced to a syrup consistency. Add the stock and reduce the heat to a low simmer. Cook for 30 minutes or until the pumpkin is very soft.

For safety, allow the soup to cool a little and then transfer the soup to a high-speed blender and purée the soup. Pass through a fine sieve – the finer the texture, the better it will taste. Season with extra salt to taste. If desired, serve the soup in a hollowed-out pumpkin.

Candied pumpkin

— Serves 8

I first came across this recipe from a chef from Argentina, where it is a home staple. I thought it delicious and unusual and it may have made the menu. It dropped out of sight for a while until we had a young Turkish chef cook for us. He made it as a dessert snack but explained they (the Turkish people) actually ate it for breakfast. I couldn't stop eating it. The sweet and sour flavour with an almost beguiling crunch ended up causing me to get my hand slapped as I reached for more. We did have customers to serve.

---

430 g (15 oz) lime powder (builder's hydrated lime)

1 large butternut pumpkin (squash)

2.7 kg (6 lb) caster (superfine) sugar

15 g (½ oz) citric acid

Carefully mix the lime powder with 5 litres (170 fl oz/20 cups) water. Place in the refrigerator overnight. The lime will sink to the bottom of the container.

Decant the water and discard the lime sludge.

Peel the pumpkin, cut it in half and use a large spoon to remove the seeds. Cut the pumpkin into even-sized pieces, about 3 cm (1¼ in).

Place the pumpkin in the lime water and leave overnight.

In a large saucepan, bring 3.5 litres (118 fl oz/14 cups) fresh water and the sugar to the boil. Remove from the heat and cool to room temperature.

Put the pumpkin in a saucepan and cover it with the sugar syrup. Ensure the pumpkin is completely covered. Cook for 2½ hours on a low simmer. Do not let the syrup boil. Every 30 minutes, remove the pumpkin from the syrup with a slotted spoon, drain for 2 minutes, then return it to the syrup.

After 2½ hours, add the citric acid and cook for another 2 minutes.

Remove from the heat and cool the pumpkin in the syrup in the refrigerator.

Before serving, allow the pumpkin to come to room temperature and then drain off any excess syrup.

For more information on lime powder, see page 13.

Pumpkin consommé
— Serves 6

This looks like a rather technical recipe, but it is no more or less so than a traditional pumpkin soup. I include it because of its delightful clarity of flavour. It is pure essence of pumpkin and a very elegant and refined rendering of a commonplace vegetable. Serve it in a china cup as an introduction to dinner, or use in place of a traditional consommé with, maybe, tiny pumpkin tortellini.

---

2 large jap (kent) pumpkins (winter squash)

5% lemon juice

5% orange juice

0.18% agar agar

0.35% xanthan gum

Remove the skin from the pumpkins and juice the flesh.

Weigh the juice and add 5% of its weight in lemon juice and 5% of its weight in orange juice.

Pass the juice mix through a sieve and weigh it again. Add 0.18% of its weight in agar agar and whisk it into the juice.

In a saucepan over medium heat, bring the juice to a high simmer and whisk for 1 minute. Pour the juice into a bowl set over an ice bath to cool.

Once cool, whisk the juice to break up the jellied structure that has formed.

Pass the mixture through an oil filter or piece of muslin (cheesecloth).

Using a hand-held blender, thicken the clarified juice with 0.35% of its total weight in xanthan gum, being careful not to incorporate too much air into the mix.

Pass the mixture through a fine sieve again before serving. Store in the refrigerator for up to 3 days or freeze for later use.

The clarification with agar agar is an excellent strategy for clarifying fruit and vegetable juices while maintaining their freshness and integrity.

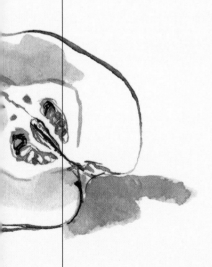

CHAPTER TWENTY-SIX

—

Quince

Quince jelly

— Makes 3 × 500 ml (1 lb 2 oz) jars

The beauty of this is in its colour. The late great Henri Jayer, one of Burgundy's most famous winemakers, said that good Pinot Noir should shine like a ruby. I think he would have approved of this. Quince are full of bitter tannins to protect them from animal and insect attack – a different approach from their cousins in the rose family. Under slow cooking these tannins or phenolic compounds react with oxygen to form anthocyanins. Anthocyanins create the vivid ruby reds for our jelly – just to explain a little of the science behind the magic.

1.5 kg (3 lb 5 oz) sugar

2.25 kg (5 lb) quince

juice of 1 lemon

Put 2.5 litres (85 fl oz/10 cups) water and the sugar in a 4 litre (135 fl oz/16 cup) saucepan and bring to the boil. Reduce the heat to a low simmer.

Quarter and core the quince, adding the pieces to the saucepan as they are cut, along with the cores and seeds. Cook over medium heat until the quince are soft and light pink, around 3 hours.

Strain the liquid through a fine sieve. Reserve the quince for another use, discarding the cores and seeds.

Return the quince syrup to a clean saucepan. Juice the lemon and add both the juice and the squeezed lemon to the quince syrup and cook on a low simmer until the temperature reaches 110°C (230°F) and is a ruby red colour.

Sterilise three 500 ml (17 fl oz/2 cup) preserving jars. Pour the hot syrup into the jars and close the lid. Invert the jars to create a seal and leave to cool. This will last for 3 months or more.

Roasted quince

— Serves 4

Quince is an incredible fruit where, under the influence of languid heat, it transforms completely from something sour, astringent and inedible to a soft, perfumed, rose-coloured delight. It is an ancient fruit tied to ancient cultures. Adam and Eve's apple was more likely a quince. This recipe is not too different from one made in a Roman kitchen, with its use of honey and spices.

---

4 large quince

400 g (14 oz) brown sugar

3 tablespoons honey

juice and zest of 1 lemon

juice and zest of 1 orange

2 star anise

3 cloves

1 cinnamon stick

2 bay leaves

Preheat the oven to 160°C (320°F).

Cut the quince in half and place them, cut side down, in a stainless steel or ceramic baking dish. Cover with the sugar, honey, citrus juice and zest and 300 ml (10 fl oz) water. Add the star anise, cloves, cinnamon stick and bay leaves, cover the dish with foil and cook for 2 hours.

Remove the foil and cook for a further 1–2 hours, until the quince are soft and a deep red colour. Serve warm.

Serve with home-made vanilla ice cream, packet custard or roast pork.

Poached quince

— Serves 8

Why another quince recipe you ask? I guess it's to show their versatility with even a subtle variation in the cooking method. Cooking in syrup like this gives the deep crimson hues most people associate with the fruit. The combination of concentrated sugar and acidity cause the reaction in colour. This is a great recipe to preserve in jars after cooking and prolong the bounty of the season. With our trees at home it was always a battle between us and nature as the fruit ripened and advertised its whereabouts.

---

1 kg (2 lb 3 oz) caster (superfine) sugar

5 juniper berries

3 star anise

3 cloves

1 vanilla bean, halved

zest and juice of 1 lemon

4 large quince

Bring the sugar, 2 litres (68 fl oz/8 cups) water, the spices and vanilla to the boil in a saucepan.

Remove the pan from the heat and add the lemon zest and juice.

Peel the quince and cut them into quarters, removing the core. As each piece is cut and cored, place it into the sugar syrup to prevent oxidisation.

Return the pan to the heat with a circle of baking paper on top of the liquid and cook the quince on a low simmer for approximately 3 hours, until they are a deep ruby red colour. Allow to cool in the syrup in the refrigerator.

Keep the syrup for the next batch of quince for a deeper flavour and colour.

Left to right: Roasted quince
(page 212); Poached quince
(page 213)

CHAPTER TWENTY-SEVEN

—

Rabbit

Rabbit rillettes

— *Serves 8*

I heard the term 'underground mutton' many times from my father and grandfather, which was a rather oblique reference to food shortages and our troubles in the Great Depression and book-end world wars. Rabbit was for the poor and its reputation took many decades to recover. I remember trapping rabbits, shooting rabbits and Myxomatosis, but I can't remember eating rabbits. I was first introduced to the idea of rillettes through the post-war writings of Elizabeth David. She wrote evocatively of the sunny French Mediterranean, its noble peasant cuisine and how it was an effective tonic for her country recovering from the Second World War and in the middle of rationing. I also read about it in the Roux Brothers' French Country Cooking and Richard Olney's Simple French Food. This recipe emanates from those readings.

---

1 small wild rabbit

300 g (10½ oz) diced pork shoulder

100 g (3½ oz) coarse salt

500 g (1 lb 2 oz) duck fat

1 garlic bulb

3 cloves

1 star anise

6 bay leaves

Remove the front and hind legs from the rabbit. Cut the body into four pieces across the backbone with a heavy knife.

Put the rabbit, pork and salt in a large bowl and mix well. Place in the refrigerator for 12 hours.

Remove from the refrigerator and rinse away the salt under running water.

In a heavy casserole over medium heat, melt the duck fat. Add the meat and the remaining ingredients, except the bay leaves. Cook very slowly over low heat until the meat starts to come away from the bone and the pork starts to fall apart, about 2–3 hours. Remove the meat from the casserole.

Strain the fat and cook it in a saucepan over low heat to evaporate any water. Discard the spices.

Shred the meat using two forks and add some of the fat to moisten it.

Transfer the meat to a suitable receptacle, like a wide-mouthed mason jar or terracotta dish, pressing down on the meat to make it as flat as possible. Garnish the surface with the bay leaves. Cover the surface with 1 cm (½ in) of the reserved fat. Place in the refrigerator until firm and opaque.

The rillettes can be eaten after 24 hours, but is far better after a number of weeks. Store for up to 2 months.

Rabbit terrine

— Serves 8–10

This recipe was adapted from a recipe by the great Gaston Lenôtre, one of France's greatest pâtissiers and chef–entrepeneur founder of the restaurant, catering, retail and cooking school empire, LeNôtre. M. Lenôtre took the savoir-faire of French country cooking and turned it into high-art retail. This recipe eschews the fancy retail garnish of high street Paris and strips it back to its peasant heart, the Sauternes the only thing perhaps belying its origin.

---

1 × 1.5 kg (3 lb 5 oz) rabbit, including heart, liver and kidneys

200 g (7 oz) chicken livers

700 g (1 lb 9 oz) skinless, boneless chicken thighs, diced

800 g (1 lb 12 oz) diced pork shoulder

400 g (14 oz) diced pork back fat

2 celery stalks

2 eggs

200 g (7 oz/2 cups) rolled (porridge) oats

300 ml (10 fl oz) Sauternes

120 g (4½ oz) wholegrain mustard

1 bunch of tarragon, chopped

25 g (1 oz) salt

2 teaspoons smoked paprika

1 teaspoon freshly ground coriander seeds

1 teaspoon freshly ground white pepper

cornichons to serve (optional)

Debone the rabbit and chop it into even-sized pieces.

Put the rabbit, including its heart, liver and kidneys, the chicken livers, thigh meat, pork shoulder, pork back fat and celery through a coarse mincer (grinder).

Put the minced meat and celery in a bowl and add the eggs, oats, Sauternes, mustard, tarragon, salt and spices and mix thoroughly with your hands.

Layer a traditional ceramic terrine mould (with a lid) with two layers of plastic wrap, making sure the wrap overhangs on all sides.

Put the mixture in the mould – you should have enough to protrude above the top by 1 cm (½ in) or so. Wrap the terrine tightly in the overhanging plastic wrap and put the lid on. Allow to rest for 1 hour.

Preheat the oven to 160°C (320°F).

Place the terrine in a bain-marie (water bath) so the water comes halfway up the sides of the terrine. Cook for 1 hour 20 minutes with the lid on, until the terrine reaches a core temperature of 68°C (154°F).

When cooked, refrigerate for 24 hours with a 750 g (1 lb 11 oz) weight directly on top of the pâté. Serve at 10–14°C (50–57°F) with the cornichons, if desired.

Rabbit with cashews and seaweed
— *Serves 4*

To me, rabbit has an almost iodine flavour of the ocean. I know of classic and traditional rabbit recipes with snails and whelks, so it is no stretch that I paired it with wakame. This is one of the first original recipes of Marque and shows its age in the use of an imported ingredient. Our ethos, if that is not too big a word, changed and became a servant to the bounty of our delightful island. The wakame we used is no longer imported due to the natural and human disaster that is Fukushima.

---

1 × 1.5 kg (3 lb 5 oz) rabbit

30 ml (1 fl oz) olive oil

50 ml (1¾ fl oz) dry vermouth

200 ml (7 fl oz) dry white wine

500 ml (17 fl oz/2 cups) chicken stock

100 g (3½ oz) butter

50 g (1¾ oz/⅓ cup) plain (all-purpose) flour

1 large white onion, thinly sliced

2 celery stalks, thinly sliced

20 g (¾ oz) dried wakame (seaweed)

100 g (3½ oz) raw cashew nuts

1 teaspoon sea salt

1 teaspoon freshly ground white pepper

Remove the hind legs and shoulders from the rabbit with a sharp knife. Use a heavy knife to chop through the rabbit, just above the pelvis. Do the same just behind the neck.

Use sharp kitchen scissors to remove the belly flap from the loin right through the ribs. Use the neck, tail and belly flap for the stock.

Using a heavy knife, cut the loin section into four pieces across the backbone.

Place a frying pan over high heat and add the olive oil. Brown the rabbit trimmings. Add the vermouth and wine and cook until reduced to a syrup. Cover with the chicken stock, reduce the heat and simmer for 40 minutes.

Strain the stock and reserve. Discard the bones.

Heat the butter in a large flameproof casserole over medium heat.

Dredge the rabbit pieces in the flour then brown them on all sides in the butter. Remove the meat from the dish. Add the onion and celery to the casserole and cook until the onion is golden. Add the rabbit in a single layer, then add the wakame, cashew nuts, salt and pepper. Pour over the stock and cover with a circle of baking paper. Simmer very gently for 45 minutes, or until the meat is just starting to part from the bone. Adjust the seasoning, if required, and serve.

This is also delicious with fresh sea urchin as a garnish. If you live near the coast, use freshly harvested edible varieties of seaweed. In season substitute young almonds for the cashew nuts.

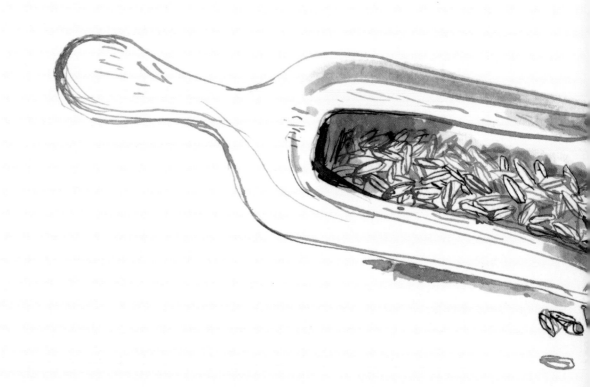

CHAPTER TWENTY-EIGHT

—

Rice

Chirashi sushi

— Serves 4–6

*The Japanese word **chirashi** means 'scattered'. This is a home-style dish to share. Serve the rice on a platter and scatter fish (raw or cooked), vegetables, sprouts, seaweed, boiled eggs and/or any additional ingredients of your choice. It is a delicious brunch dish and readily adaptable to what you have available. If you live near a fish market, as I do, this is the perfect framework for the less noble fish that are only brilliant when fresh out of the sea.*

---

440 g (15½ oz/2 cups) Japanese short-grain white rice

50 ml (1¾ fl oz) sake

500 ml (17 fl oz/2 cups) filtered water

100 ml (3½ fl oz) Japanese rice vinegar

1 teaspoon salt

15 g (½ oz) caster (superfine) sugar

Put the rice in the saucepan it will be cooked in and cover with clear, cool water. Swirl the rice gently around with your hand in the pan to remove the loose starch. Drain and repeat four or five times, until the water is clear and no longer milky. Drain completely then add the sake and filtered water. Leave the rice to soak for 20 minutes to achieve a better texture.

Place the saucepan over high heat and bring to the boil. Reduce the heat to a very low simmer, cover and cook for 15 minutes. Turn off the heat and leave the rice to steam in the saucepan for 20 minutes.

In a small saucepan over medium heat, mix together the rice vinegar, salt and sugar. Bring to the boil to dissolve the sugar and salt then remove the pan from the heat.

Put the rice in a large mixing bowl (preferably wooden) and pour over the vinegar mixture. Use a wooden spoon to stir it through, but do not mash the rice. Serve with the accompaniments of your choice.

Red rice pilaf

— Serves 6

Red rice is wholegrain rice with a deep red husk, grown in Italy and France. It is somewhat like wild rice in texture and has a complex, sweet, nutty, sticky character and brings an entirely different dimension to a 'pilaf'. You can use basmati for this dish if you like, but it's always worth the bother to try something different. The deep-fried eggs are a South East Asian thing that I thought would suit the dish in taste and texture.

---

1 red onion, finely diced

½ celery stalk, finely diced

1 garlic clove, finely chopped

2 tablespoons virgin olive oil

1 teaspoon coriander seeds

1 teaspoon cumin seeds

1 teaspoon white peppercorns

1 teaspoon sea salt

30 g (1 oz) butter

250 g (9 oz) red rice

750 ml (25½ fl oz/3 cups) chicken stock

3 × 1 cm (1¼ × ½ in) piece orange zest

1 cinnamon stick

1 thyme sprig

1 fresh bay leaf

1 litre (34 fl oz/4 cups) rice bran oil

6 eggs

Preheat the oven to 160°C (320°F).

In a heavy-based, ovenproof frying pan over medium heat, sweat the onion, celery and garlic in the olive oil until soft.

Using a mortar and pestle, grind the coriander, cumin, peppercorns and salt to a fine powder.

Sauté the vegetables in the butter and then add the spices. Stir to combine then add the rice, stock, orange zest, cinnamon, thyme and bay leaf. Bring to a simmer.

Cut a circle of baking paper to fit inside the pan and use this to cover the rice. Transfer the pan to the oven and bake for 55 minutes.

When the rice is nearly cooked, heat the rice bran oil in a 2 litre (68 fl oz/8 cup) saucepan to 170°C (340°F). Carefully break the eggs into the oil and fry each for around 1 minute. The white should be like crisp golden lace and the yolks soft and runny. Use a slotted spoon to remove the eggs as they are cooked and transfer to paper towel to drain.

Season the eggs with a little sea salt and serve them on top of the rice in a serving dish.

Risotto milanese

— Serves 6

Risotto is one of those traditional dishes so surrounded by rules and lore that it's hard for any two people to agree on what is 'correct'. These are the basic criteria for a good risotto and in no particular order of importance: the correct rice, the correct pan, the correct base recipe, the correct toasting of the rice, the correct way to stir, the correct degree of patience, whether to add fat at the end or not, and when it is ready it should create a 'wave' (how big this wave is, is a matter of dispute). This is one version and it's good and delicious and some people would agree. As the Romans would say, **De gustibus non est disputandum** *('in matters of taste, there are no disputes').*

---

2 litres (68 fl oz/8 cups) beef broth

100 g (3½ oz) bone marrow

3 French shallots, finely chopped

240 g (8½ oz) carnaroli rice

40 saffron threads

100 ml (3½ fl oz) dry white wine

1 teaspoon sea salt

3 tablespoons grated Parmigiano Reggiano

20 g (¾ oz) butter

1 teaspoon freshly ground white pepper

Heat the broth in a saucepan over medium heat. Set aside and keep warm.

Heat the bone marrow in a 4 litre (135 fl oz/16 cup) saucepan over medium heat until it melts. Add the shallot and cook, stirring, until it is soft, about 3 minutes. Add the rice and cook for 2 minutes to 'toast' it. Add the saffron then the wine. Cook until the wine has reduced and evaporated. Add the salt. Add the reserved stock, 125 ml (4 fl oz/½ cup) at a time, stirring until each addition is absorbed before adding more.

Cook, stirring often, until the rice is tender and creamy, about 20–22 minutes. Stir in the parmesan, butter and pepper and adjust the salt if necessary.

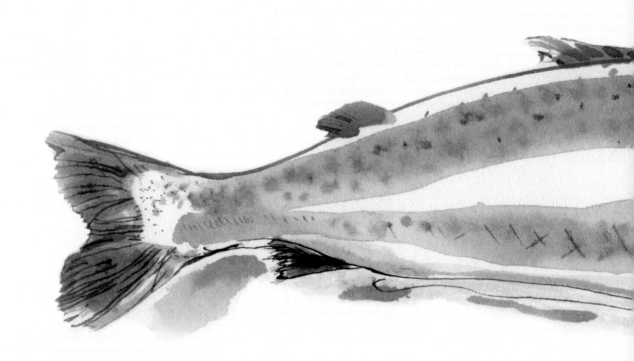

CHAPTER TWENTY-NINE

—

Salmon

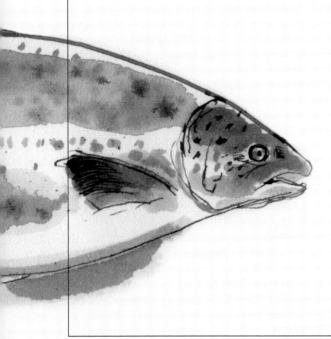

Confit salmon

— Serves 6

Something happened to salmon between the time I first saw a picture of one in a bear's paw and it appearing in great slimy orange piles at the supermarket deli counter. If there ever was a case of familiarity breeding contempt, this was it. This is the banality of mass production. The fish itself is not at fault, it's the victim. There are many fine producers of farmed fish and the quality chain is maintained through quality suppliers. These are the fish we are talking about. There is no point in putting lipstick on a pig.

---

1 kg (2 lb 3 oz) salmon fillet

1 teaspoon black peppercorns

½ teaspoon juniper berries

20 g (¾ oz) sea salt

10 g (¼ oz) raw (demerara) sugar

50 ml (1¾ fl oz) extra-virgin olive oil

Skin and pin-bone the salmon fillet.

Coarsely grind the peppercorns and juniper berries in a spice grinder, or use a mortar and pestle. Mix in the salt and sugar.

Preheat the oven to 50°C (120°F).

Rub the fish with the olive oil and then gently coat the fish with the spices, making sure to coat both sides evenly. Wrap tightly in plastic wrap and place on a rack in the oven for 25 minutes.

Refrigerate overnight before serving.

This is best served at room temperature with a salad of mixed leaf chicory (endive) and new season's olive oil.

Salmon boudin

— Serves 4

This was one of the first recipes on the menu of our first restaurant in 1986. It was served gently fried in butter with braised lentils du Puy and thyme. I'm not sure where the recipe came from, but it stands the test of time on remaking. It's a little pale pink DeLorean to a time when there was no internet. This is delicious garnished with caviar and rosé Champagne.

---

200 g (7 oz) salmon fillet

8 g (¼ oz) table salt

½ teaspoon freshly ground white pepper

¼ teaspoon mace

200 ml (7 fl oz) pouring (single/light) cream, cold

1 m (3 ft 3 in) natural or synthetic pork casing

Cut the salmon into 3 cm (1¼ in) cubes and refrigerate. (The cream and salmon must be very cold for the best results.)

Also put the bowl and blade of a food processor in the freezer for 1 hour prior to preparing the fish.

Put the chilled salmon in the food processor and blend to a fine paste. Add the salt and spices. With the processor running, pour in the cream and stop when it's just incorporated.

Use a spatula to push the mousse through a fine sieve.

Rinse the casing with running water and drain. Tie one end of the sausage casing and feed the casing onto the sausage funnel of your mincer (grinder). Pour the mousse into the funnel. When the casing is full, tie and twist it into 15 cm (6 in) segments. Tie each segment with a piece of string to stop it unwinding, making sure the sausage is a little slack to allow for expansion during cooking and to prevent bursting.

Prick each sausage four or five times with a fine needle to eliminate air bubbles.

Heat a saucepan of water to 80–82°C (176–180°F). Cook the sausages in the water for about 1 hour, with a wet tea towel (dish towel) on top to ensure the boudin are under the water.

Carefully remove the sausages from the cooking water (they are prone to bursting at this stage) and cool them in iced water.

Refrigerate until required or, if preferred, they can be cold-smoked. (See page 135 for directions on smoking.)

To serve, remove the skin and gently fry them in butter until golden. Warm them through in a 60°C (140°F) oven.

The temperatures are all important here. Pay heed to them.

Wind-dried salmon

— Serves 8–10

'Wind-drying' salmon is something long associated with the people of northern Canada and Alaska where wild fish are caught, dried and shared. We approximate the wild with farmed fish and our wine cellar. It doesn't have the romance, but we also don't have to guard against bear attack. The cool, moderately dry ageing environment allows a slow and deliberate evaporation of moisture from the fish, concentrating flavour, colour and texture.

2 cleaned salmon fillets (around 1 kg/2 lb 3 oz each), skin on

80 g (2¾ oz) fine sea salt

45 g (1½ oz) caster (superfine) sugar

wood chips for smoking (hickory for preference)

25 g (1 oz) brown sugar

Begin 15 days ahead.

Cover a work surface with plastic wrap and place the salmon fillets, skin side down, next to each other on the wrap.

Combine the salt and sugar and gently rub the mixture on the flesh side of one salmon fillet. Carefully place the second salmon fillet on top of the first, flesh sides together. Press down gently.

Using the plastic wrap, tightly wrap the salmon fillets together. Put them on a large tray to support the fish and place in the refrigerator to cure for 4 days, turning the parcel over daily.

On the fourth day, gently rinse the salt and sugar off each fillet under cold running water. Pat the fish dry with paper towel.

Place the fillets, flesh side up, on a wire rack on a baking tray and place the tray on the top rack of a cold oven. Leave the oven door open.

Cut a piece of foil into a 15 cm (6 in) square. Mould the foil to form a well and pour in the brown sugar. Put the foil well in the centre of an old ovenproof frying pan and surround it with wood chips. Turn the heat to high and allow the wood chips to catch fire. This will take around 3 minutes.

Once the chips are alight, carefully shake the pan to disperse the chips and allow even burning.

Once all the chips are alight, carefully place another pan of the same size on top of the first pan, to snuff out the flames.

Place the pans inside the oven on the bottom shelf. Remove the top pan and quickly close the oven door, trapping the smoke inside. Leave for 5 minutes or until all the smoke has dissipated. Repeat the smoking process three times.

Once the cured salmon has been smoked, place the fillets back together and tightly wrap them in plastic wrap. Rest for 1 day to allow the smoke to penetrate the fish.

On the following day, carefully and firmly tie the fillets through the tail end with butcher's string. Hang to dry in a climate-controlled area, at around 17°C (63°F), for 10 days.

Try kingfish (yellowtail), albacore tuna or mackerel using the same technique.

Left to right: Salmon boudin
(page 236); Wind-dried salmon
(page 237)

–

CHAPTER THIRTY

Tomatoes

Tomato soup

— Serves 6

This is a dish to make in full summer when tomatoes are abundant, cheap and very ripe. You can make it with tinned tomatoes or passata but you may be in gross danger of missing the point. Grow your own, visit the markets, cook. Get out of the supermarket cycle. No one is so 'time poor' that they can't find time to cook a simple soup. The process delivers far more than the sum of its ingredients. It is good for the soul.

---

1 onion, coarsely chopped

2 garlic cloves, chopped

100 ml (3½ fl oz) olive oil

¼ teaspoon dried chilli flakes

1 kg (2 lb 3 oz) ripe cooking tomatoes, coarsely chopped

2 thyme sprigs

1 bay leaf

2 basil leaves

1 marjoram sprig

1 oregano sprig

2 teaspoons sea salt

1 teaspoon raw (demerara) sugar

¼ teaspoon ground star anise

½ teaspoon freshly ground white pepper

3 teaspoons potato starch

In a large saucepan over medium–high heat, sauté the onion and garlic in the olive oil until lightly golden. Add the chilli, cook a little more, then add the tomatoes.

Tie the herbs into a small bundle with butcher's string and then add them to the pan. Add the salt, sugar, star anise and pepper. Stir well and cover the pan with a lid. Cook on a low simmer for 1½ hours.

Remove the herbs. Leave the soup to cool, then blend it to a fine purée with a hand-held blender.

Using the back of a ladle, pass the soup through a very fine sieve into a clean saucepan over medium heat.

Mix the potato starch with 2 tablespoons water and add this slurry to the soup. Stir the soup until it thickens. Adjust the seasoning if required.

❈

Processing very hot soup in a blender can cause a steam 'explosion'. Be warned!

Tomato and parmesan marshmallow

— Serves 10

The curious thing about this is that it is pure white. When we think of tomato we think of red. The colour and the flavour are so closely linked that when we bite into something white and it tastes intensely of tomato there is a moment of shock as the brain makes sense of it. It is just parmesan and tomato but the form has rendered it unrecognisable. The important thing, though, is that it tastes intensely of both ingredients and is delicious.

---

3 French shallots

3 garlic cloves

2 small red chillies

1 small bunch of basil, leaves picked

4 thyme sprigs, leaves picked

4 kg (8 lb 13 oz) ripe roma (plum) tomatoes, quartered and cored

2 tablespoons sherry vinegar

1 tablespoon sea salt

2 teaspoons caster (superfine) sugar

50 g (1¾ oz) titanium-strength gelatine leaves

250 g (9 oz) parmesan

Put the shallots, garlic, chilli and herbs in a blender and mix on high speed. Add the tomatoes, sherry vinegar, salt and sugar and blend to a coarse purée.

Suspend an oil filter or piece of muslin (cheesecloth) over a bowl. Pour in the tomato pulp and let it drip overnight to collect the clear tomato juice.

Soak the gelatine in iced water until soft.

To make the marshmallow, measure out 750 ml (25½ fl oz/3 cups) of the tomato juice. Warm one-third of the tomato juice in a saucepan over medium heat.

Squeeze any excess water from the gelatine and stir it into the tomato juice in the pan until dissolved.

Pass the mixture through a fine sieve into the cold tomato juice and refrigerate for 3 hours or until set.

Chill a mixing bowl in the refrigerator until cold.

Once set, transfer the jelly to the chilled mixing bowl. Whip using an electric mixer on high speed until the jelly resembles stiff meringue.

Spread the whipped jelly in a chilled 3 cm (1¼ in) deep tray lined with plastic wrap – work quickly as it will start to set. Refrigerate until fully set.

While it is setting, finely grate the parmesan. A microplane is best for this.

Tip the marshmallow out onto a cutting board and cut it into 3 cm (1¼ in) cubes. Gently roll the cubes in the grated cheese and serve immediately.

Stuffed caramelised tomatoes
— *Serves 6*

An invention of the great Alain Passard, this remains one of the great tomato dishes of the restaurant world. Even at some 20 years old, the idea of serving tomato for dessert is a cause of consternation to most people. The tomato is in fact a fruit, is sweet and tastes like Christmas. Where is the downside?

6 small–medium vine-ripened
tomatoes, vine still attached

TOMATO STUFFING

zest and juice of 1 lemon

zest and juice of 1 orange, plus
200 ml (7 fl oz) orange juice

2 pears, peeled and cut into
3 mm (⅛ in) dice

2 apples, peeled and cut into
3 mm (⅛ in) dice

1 pineapple, peeled and cut into
3 mm (⅛ in) dice

50 g (1¾ oz) slivered almonds,
finely chopped

50 g (1¾ oz/⅓ cup) pistachio nuts,
finely chopped

½ bunch of mint, leaves picked
and shredded

50 g (1¾ oz/⅓ cup) currants

2 teaspoons ground star anise

1 teaspoon ground cloves

1 vanilla bean, split and
seeds scraped

500 g (1 lb 2 oz) sugar

Blanch the tomatoes in boiling water and refresh immediately in iced water. Remove the skins but retain the stem in place.

Cut a small 'cone' out of the bottom of the tomatoes. Using a small melon baller, remove the tomato flesh and seeds. Place the tomatoes on a wire rack set over a tray, along with the cone pieces, in the refrigerator overnight to dry them out.

Preheat the oven to 70°C (160°F).

To make the stuffing, put the citrus zest and juice (except the 200 ml/7 fl oz orange juice) in a large bowl. Add the pear, apple and pineapple to the citrus juice. Add the nuts, mint, currants and spices and combine.

In a heavy-based saucepan over medium heat, bring the sugar and 150 ml (5 fl oz) water to 121°C (250°F). Add the stuffing mixture and simmer for 3 minutes.

Pass the mixture through a fine sieve and set aside.

Cool the fruit mixture and store in the refrigerator.

Pour the reserved liquid back in the saucepan and return the pan to the stove top over medium heat. Reduce the liquid down to a dark caramel. Remove the pan from the heat and carefully pour in the 200 ml (7 fl oz) orange juice to stop the cooking process. Pass through a fine sieve.

Preheat the oven to 150°C (300°F).

Once dry, stuff the blanched tomatoes with the filling, then replace each cone piece. Cover with the tomato caramel and place in the oven. Baste every 15–20 minutes until the tomatoes are caramelised, about 2 hours.

CHAPTER THIRTY-ONE

—

Yoghurt

Yoghurt and white chocolate ganache

— *Serves 4*

White chocolate's dirty secret is that it is not really chocolate, commonly being made of cocoa butter, sugar and milk solids. Some cheaper examples don't even use cocoa butter, but vegetable or animal fats. I actually don't like white chocolate that much. Not because it's an imposter but mostly as it is way too sweet. I hate that cloying, sugar burn. Having said this, it can be quite good to cook with when using it as a base ingredient. This is a very simple recipe and relies on the quality and ratio of the ingredients. The tart lactic acidity of the yoghurt cuts the sugar rush and renders it delicious.

---

225 g (8 oz) best-quality white couverture chocolate

120 ml (4 fl oz) pouring (single/light) cream (35% milk fat)

180 g (6½ oz) Greek-style yoghurt

Finely chop the white chocolate and put it in a heatproof bowl with the cream.

Melt the chocolate over a double boiler, ensuring the water doesn't touch the base of the bowl and the temperature of the chocolate does not rise above 50°C (122°F). Cool slightly.

Whisk in the yoghurt until fully incorporated then pass the ganache through a fine sieve.

Place in the refrigerator for 1 hour or until set.

Serve with berries or blood orange.

Yoghurt sorbet

— Serves 4

A good sorbet relies on the correct ratio of cold, base ingredient and sugar. Many years ago I remember going to a flea market in Sydney. It was about 1985 but most stallholders still seemed trapped in the age of Aquarius. In between the candle stalls, bhaji sellers and dream catchers was a guy forcing frozen bananas through a wheatgrass juicer. The result was fabulous frozen banana sausage of exceptional texture and flavour. Genius.

1 titanium-strength gelatine leaf

iced water

200 g (7 oz) sugar

250 g (9 oz/1 cup) Greek-style yoghurt

30 ml (1 fl oz) lemon juice

Soak the gelatine in iced water until completely soft.

Bring 350 ml (12 fl oz) water and the sugar to the boil in a saucepan over medium heat.

Squeeze any excess water from the gelatine and whisk it into the sugar syrup until it has dissolved. Remove the pan from the heat and allow the mixture to cool.

Whisk in the yoghurt and lemon juice then pass the mixture through a fine sieve.

Churn in an ice cream machine according to the manufacturer's instructions.

Home-made yoghurt
— *Makes 4 × 500 ml (17 fl oz/2 cup) jars*

Take your time, slow down, breathe, relax, make some yoghurt. Pull back from the passive consumer cycle and taste the difference. Use the last of this batch of yoghurt to make your next batch. You can do this until you die at a ripe old age.

---

2 litres (68 fl oz/8 cups) organic full-cream (whole) milk

200 g (7 oz) live culture yoghurt (thermophilic bacteria), at room temperature

Put four 500 ml (17 fl oz/2 cup) mason jars and their lids in the oven. Turn the oven to 100°C (210°F) and sterilise the jars for 20 minutes. Turn off the heat and leave the jars in the oven to cool.

Half-fill a 3–4 litre (101–135 fl oz/12–16 cup) saucepan with water and bring to a low simmer. Place a large stainless steel bowl over the pan of water and add the milk. Stir constantly with a wooden spoon until the mixture reaches a temperature of 82°C (180°F).

Fill an insulated cooler with hot tap water.

Remove the milk from the heat and cool to 49°C (120°F). Whisk in the live culture yoghurt.

Carefully fill the jars with the mixture and put on the lids.

Drain the insulated cooler and put the jars inside. Put the lid on the cooler and keep in a warm place for up to 8 hours. The longer and slower the incubation, the tangier and thicker the yoghurt. If you can maintain the temperature at 43°C (109°F) for 24 hours, you will have some very fine yoghurt.

Index

—

Page references followed by 'n' indicate notes at the foot of the page.

ACKNOWLEDGEMENTS

—

This book is an amalgamation of much effort
and passion for craft.

Thank you to my long-suffering and patient publisher, Hardie Grant, who I suspect knew I'd spent the advance well before any thought or commitment to paper. Thank you to Jane Willson, my publisher, for her acerbic wit, the confidence that this would actually happen and knowing just how to prod me into action; Ariana Klepac for arranging my random thoughts with precision and kindness; Robin Cowcher for the delightful original illustrations; and the design team led by Mark Campbell for realising the look – it's perfect guys! And I'd like to thank Myffy Rigby, for she knows my black heart is only a façade.

On the ground for the shoot at Marque we had an amazing core team that 'got it done': Lauren Eldridge for your organisational skill, culinary talent and withering eye for detail; Nobu Lee who produced a veritable tonne of beautiful food while still running the daily operation of a busy restaurant; Chris Boersma, my talented floor manager, for allowing and facilitating the integration of a photo studio into our daily life; Geraldine Muñoz, patience and charm personified and the brunt of much teasing, styled the fuck out of the brief and we were never left wondering what we needed to do next; and Petrina Tinslay, who brings a gentle charm, strength and integrity to any project she is associated with. I was honoured she chose to do this one. Petrina your work is beautiful.

—

Mark Best, taste-maker and culinary wild man

So just who is Mark Best?

A few years ago, I wrote in a review of Mark's Sydney restaurant Marque that a particular mainstay on the menu was a guaranteed gag-maker. It was the crab custard with frozen foie gras. Don't get me wrong, a lot of people love this dish, but I will cross town to not be in the same room with it. Lo, the next time I turn up at the restaurant it appears in front of me again. And again on every subsequent visit. You've got to admire a man with that much tenacity. Or at least a man that bloody minded that he would insist on serving a customer something they didn't just find unappealing, but actively loathed.

Mark Best isn't just a taste-maker, he makes other people taste.

He's sensitive and smart, sharp and creative. He's an impressive portrait photographer, capturing both the chefs in his kitchen and those around him with an interesting mix of gloss and grit. And, most importantly, he can also successfully rewire a power point thanks to his past life as an electrician, working the mines in Western Australia. Few chefs can boast such a broad palette of skills, but Mark Best doesn't boast at all.

For a man with such a restless and electric mind, Mark Best has a very still countenance. The Patrick Bateman of the Sydney dining scene, you just get the feeling that any moment he'll pause telling that after-hours blue joke, pull out a man's still-beating heart, slice it, sear it and finish with the punch line. Does that give the right impression of Mark Best? Maybe. Or maybe he'll just cut this bit out. I hope not.

In the decade I've worked as a restaurant critic in Sydney, I've watched Mark not so much transform in his food – his cooking has always been seasoned with a certain idiosyncratic flair – but in the way he nurtures and supports other up-and-coming chefs. He's now had three Josephine Pignolet Award winners pass through his kitchen. All three have gone on to great things.

He's been a star on the World's 50 Best Restaurants list. He's made and ridden media waves across the globe, and travelled broadly. Not content to simply run one of the country's most progressive fine dining restaurants, the chef decided to open a bistro in Melbourne. And another in Sydney. So he can play it wild, and he can play it straight. Interestingly, through all of that, he's been a constant. His vigilance, his rigour, his sharp intellect and his insatiable need to create new things are a large part of what makes up who he is as a chef and a restaurateur.

Mark Best is one of the most independently minded cooks in Australia. He makes menus of blood, he inspires young chefs, he serves what he likes. His priority has always been to challenge. To delight is just a side effect. To truly thrill is divine.

Myffy Rigby

Published in 2016 by Hardie Grant Books

Hardie Grant Books (Australia)
Ground Floor, Building 1
658 Church Street
Richmond, Victoria 3121
www.hardiegrant.com.au

Hardie Grant Books (UK)
5th & 6th Floors
52–54 Southwark Street
London SE1 1UN
www.hardiegrant.co.uk

A Cataloguing-in-Publication entry is available from the catalogue
of the National Library of Australia at www.nla.gov.au

Best Kitchen Basics
ISBN: 9781742709802

Publishing director: Jane Willson
Project editors: Hannah Koelmeyer & Ariana Klepac
Editor: Ariana Klepac
Design manager: Mark Campbell
Designer: Murray Batten
Typesetter: Megan Ellis
Illustrator: Robin Cowcher
Photographer: Petrina Tinslay
Stylist: Geraldine Muñoz
Production manager: Todd Rechner

Hardie Grant and Mark Best would like to thank these suppliers for their
generosity with props during our photo shoot:
Marie-Hélène Clauzon and MH Ceramics; Chee Soon & Fitzgerald; The
Fortynine Studio; Aeria Country Floors; Catapult Design; and Dinosaur Designs.

Colour reproduction by Splitting Image Colour Studio

Printed in China by 1010 Printing International Limited